The Mythology Surrounding Freud and Klein

Dialog-on-Freud

Series Editor: M. Andrew Holowchak

The Dialog-on-Freud series invites authors to explore the history and practice of analytic therapies through critical analysis of and expatiation on the seminal work of Freud. It seeks books that critically scrutinize the numerous facets of Freud's work over the course of his life, that investigate how or to what extent Freud's thinking causally gave rise to the various sorts of therapies that currently exist, and that examine the relevance of Freud's thinking today for those therapies.

Titles in the Series

Cultural Therapy, by Jay Harris
How Talking Cures: Revealing Freud's Contributions to All Psychotherapies, by Lee Jaffe
The Unconscious without Freud, by Rosemarie Sand
Freud's Theory of Dreams: A Philosophico-Scientific Perspective, by Michael T. Michael
Nabakov's Mimicry of Freud: Art as Science, by Teckyoung Kwon
How Culture Runs the Brain: A Freudian View of Collective Syndromes, by Jay Evans Harris
The Mythology Surrounding Freud and Klein: Implications for Psychoanalysis, by Charlotte Schwartz

The Mythology Surrounding Freud and Klein

Implications for Psychoanalysis

Charlotte Schwartz

LEXINGTON BOOKS
Lanham • Boulder • New York • London

Published by Lexington Books
An imprint of The Rowman & Littlefield Publishing Group, Inc.
4501 Forbes Boulevard, Suite 200, Lanham, Maryland 20706
www.rowman.com

Unit A, Whitacre Mews, 26-34 Stannary Street, London SE11 4AB

British Library Cataloguing in Publication Information Available

Library of Congress Cataloging-in-Publication Data Available

ISBN 978-1-4985-6848-7 (cloth : alk. paper)
ISBN 978-1-4985-6849-4 (electronic)

∞™ The paper used in this publication meets the minimum requirements of American National Standard for Information Sciences Permanence of Paper for Printed Library Materials, ANSI/NISO Z39.48-1992.

Printed in the United States of America

To my children
Martin, Rachel, Joshua, and Lonna
and my Grandchildren
Isaac, Florise, Soren, Ethan, Theo, and Sophia

Contents

Introduction

Mythologies Surrounding Freud and Klein

Implications for Psychoanalytic Training

> "Medicine is a science of uncertainty, and an art of probablity."
> —Sir William Osler

My primary purpose in this project is to redress the distortion, and perpetuation of the myth, that Freud did not consider the "object" in psychic development, and that Klein was the "originator" of object relations theory. I am attempting to correct these fallacies by presenting a thorough study of their writings and case histories. This exegesis of Freud and Klein's thinking on the Object and the Instincts[1] is essential not only for the sake of "truth" but most important for the education of a new core of psychoanalysts. To focus on Freud's concern with the object in psychological development and the vicissitudes of instincts is to bring some clarity to how Freud viewed psychic organization and function.

Though Klein repeatedly referred to the "object," her object was in essence a phylogenetic object that was created and infused by the instincts, and only secondarily, ontogenetic. This recognition of her "drive-object" corrects a major fallacy in current psychoanalytic theory. A study of her theories shows that she was closely attuned to Freud's instinct constructs and not with the "object theorists" as has been claimed. The object that existed in the real world was rarely considered in Klein's writings.

The impact of their thinking will be studied with particular emphasis on how the distortion of Freud's theories on the "object," and Klein's theories on the "drives," influenced not only current psychoanalytic theory but an entire cadre of analysts from both the classical and the object relational schools. The claim that Freud had a significant object relation's theory, and Klein actually was a drive theorist may appear somewhat surprising for the new corpus of analysts (Skolnick, N. 1998). The challenge to the claim that Freud ignored the impact of the environment on psychological development and its influence on character structure (Horney, 1937; Guntrip, 1969b; Fairbairn, 1940, 1944, 1946) is also most pertinent to this study. To claim that Klein was a drive theorist is to provide historical accuracy and belies the beliefs of the British Object School who gave her the nom-de-plum of "originator" of object relations theory (Guntrip, 1961e, f, 1969c).

Further, a review at this point in history appears particularly important given the number of analytic institutes that negate drive constructs, claiming them unsustainable. Thus, they have established object-relations theory as the fundamental premise for psychoanalytic theory. Freud and his theoretical premises have become the subject of major criticism. He has been chastised for his supposed failure to understand the primacy of the object and object relations in psychic structure and in the treatment process (Guntrip, 1969a, b, c; Stolorow and Atwood, 1992). According to his critics, Freud's focus on energic concepts, discharge, defense, and the pleasure-unpleasure principle, rather than on object relations, had led to inadequate explanatory theories.

Fairbairn (1957) indicated: "classic libido theory would have to be transformed into a theory of development based essentially upon object relations" (31). Thus, according to Farbairn, libido does not strive for fruition of instinct need states, but rather the goal is object seeking. Guntrip (1961b), who opined that object-relations theory was the creation of Melanie Klein, indicated:

> Freud hovered between the psychology of the organism and the psychology of the person, a theory of instincts and a theory of object-relations, his theory in toto remained fundamentally oriented to biology. Thus he makes character dependent on the organic maturing of the sexual instincts rather than dealing with the sexual functioning as controlled by the extent to which character has matured in human relationships. Moreover, his radical subordination of the object to the role of mere means to the gratification of the instincts is unsatisfactory from a sociological and from a human point of view since it treats personal relationships on a subpersonal level (29).

Some twenty years later, we are again confronted by a similar critique in that Greenberg and Mitchell (1983) indicated that though the concept of object relations "originated as an inherent part of Freud's drive theory," it essentially played a minimal role conceptually in his theories (14).

Even Compton, a classical theorist who has studied Freud's work extensively (1981, 1983, 1985, a, b, 1986), stated that Freud " has also never quite resolved his equivocation about whether there is an object choice in infancy"

(1986, 573). He further indicated that "Freud's eventual un-equivocation regarding object choice is finally centered around the "Oedipus situation." However, even more glaring of error is Compton's statement that Freud's inclusion of the phallic-oedipal-castration phase in the development sequence of sexual organization was the outcome of a gradual, and seeming reluctant recognition by him of the import of "objects" in early childhood. And it only became central when in assembling various observations, especially on the male-female differentiation, that he then developed the new structural model. Object choice, as Freud used the term, however, did not apply prior to the phallic–Oedipal phase (576).

Further, that Compton (1985) refers to Freud's usage of the "Drive-Object" as solely a function of discharge does an injustice to Freud's early conceptualization of the helpless infant who turns to the object motivated by the libidinal drive. Fairbairn's drive theory as object directed is not that much different in the end result from Freud's theory of the needed object; the major difference being that Fairbairn eliminated the concept of sexual instinct from his theory.

Freud had clearly pointed to the centricity of object choice far earlier than the Oedipal situation. Furthermore, by the very failure of the Object Theorists to recognize Freud as their most significant predecessor or, in so minimizing his contribution to theories of object relations, and the primacy of the object in psychic structure, have provided a base-line for the elimination of drive theory from the literature and the treatment. Therefore, by negation or so completely minimizing the interaction between drive and object, the result is a restructured theory of psychic development (Busch, 1999). The emphasis has shifted to the manifest experience with the object and under-values the impact of drives on object relations, defense, and ego structure (Glover, 1927; Shapiro, 1990).

Klein, as one studies her work particularly from the period between 1921 and 1937 (Glover, 1945; Grossruth, 1987; Makari, 2008) shows herself as a drive theorist for whom the external environment barely enters into consideration in her case studies (Fritz, 1919; Erna, 1924; Richard, 1941). Klein minimized the actual role of the external object, particularly the mother. Her thoughts on the internalized object had reference to phantasies derived from internal drive states (1919–1935), that is, the libidinal and aggressive drives. According to Makari (1986), Klein "as time went on would pay less and less attention to an unloving or cruel environment and argue that a child's troubles were his own psychic making" (427–428). Klein's work, unquestionably, contradicts Guntrip's appellation of her as the originator of object relations theory and as the most significant ancestor of the object relational schools (1961g, 215-233). If one were to ascribe to anyone other than Freud as the "originator of object theory" then appellation should be awarded to Ferenczi (1913, 1922, 1932a, b, c) who had written a number of significant papers on the role of the object and the importance of object relationships, particularly in the analytic relationship.

Assessing Klein's theories on the object requires recognition that her treatment, clinical evaluations, and writings are fundamentally instinct theories. Though Makari (2008) stated that Klein had no real understanding of instinct in the sense that Freud meant, and that she viewed both libido and aggression "as inherently directional longings and the drives were in effect relationships" (108). Still, Klein's constant reference to drives as an inherent energic concept, and objects as phylogenetic structures must be differentiated from the reality role of the external object. Further, her adherence to the Death Instinct, its aim, particularly, in relation to early wishes of destroying the mother, and the subsequent guilt and reparation, makes it difficult to unclassify her as a drive theorist.

Therefore, to understand Fairbairn's and Guntrip's view of Freud and Klein begs the question of logic and objectivity, and raises a conundrum that almost defies understanding. Both men were important theorists, and major exponents of the British Object-Relational School that constituted the Middle Group of the British Psychoanalytic Society.

King and Steiner (1991), in their book on *The Freud-Klein Controversies—1941–1945*, alluded to the underlying struggles for power and influence that undoubtedly played a significant role in the divergent theories that had begun to develop within the British Society, especially after the arrival of Melanie Klein to England in 1926. Poland (2002) and Rangel (2004) have commented on the role by which power struggles influence theory, distort objective factors, and lead to much dissention within the psychoanalytic societies. To create a new theory, to abnegate the old, begets historical relevancy and fame. Yet, it is also possible to suggest a theory that both Guntrip and Fairbairn had a strong religious orientation and both had considered following a career in religion. Thus, they would have had an antipathy to the idea of sexual instincts as a dominant factor in human development. An object relational motif of human interaction would have provided their religious orientation with a greater sense of hopefulness and capacity for change. The sense of "personal will" could more easily overcome destructive behavior than a biological force of instinct.

Unfortunately, the misconceptions and misjudgments regarding Freud and Klein have become theoretically mythologized and have been handed down to the future generations of analysts as truisms. These myths have permeated the culture of psychoanalysis, the training institutes, and the public domain (see NY times–Daniel Goleman, 1980s). Andre Green (2000) had pointed to the damaging effects of omitting the role of sexuality and aggression as independent drive states in the curriculum of analytic institutes and has warned that this has resulted "in a narrowing the base of psychoanalytic knowledge."

Curtis (1985) and Lussier (1988) warned that the implicit result of reducing Freud's theories on the object and object relations to a minor inquiry, has made it possible to draw negative conclusions regarding the function of the drives. Concepts, such as energy, discharge, and the Pleasure Principle are regarded as principles of "limited usefulness" (Schafer, 1983) and have been replaced by theories consisting primarily of object relationships and intersubjectivity. The object has assumed the primary role in modulation of affects, and determinants of motivation, and aim.

To disprove these myths regarding Freud and Klein is the goal of this study. To establish the validity of the stated premise may appear easier to achieve than to undo what is already mentally implanted in the culture. This becomes the real challenge. A thematic and linear perspective of their work hopefully will provide the evidence that both adhered to, a not to dissimilar view on the role of instincts, their maturational process, the impact on object relations, and in the development of psychic structure.

What may appear as a surprise is that Freud (1905, 1921), more than Klein, recognized the role of the external environment on the developing object relationships and on the "maturation of the instincts" (Heimann, 1943). Perhaps a second surprise will be my assertion that Klein gave greater recognition to the Death Instinct than even Freud, particularly in early infancy. We may recall that one of the points of disagreement between Freud and Adler concerned the role of aggression. It was not until 1920 in *Beyond the Pleasure Principle* that Freud postulated aggression as an independent drive. Even then it was subsumed under the death instinct. Freud's death drive resonated with Klein who then postulated that the death drive was operative from birth. She emphasized that it was this aggression emanating from the death drive that accounts for the ambivalence and persecutory anxiety in infancy. It is clear that the death instinct for Klein posed some very important issues regarding the nature of fusion between the two drives, Eros and Thanatos, and their role in infant development.

To present Freud and Klein in isolation from some of their most important contemporary colleagues and adherents would be a mistake. History requires a context in order to understand major ideological currents, agreements and disagreements, changes and stability. Therefore, a review of some aspects of the history of psychoanalysis will be discussed. Those analysts who played a leading role in the development of psychoanalysis with Freud, and those who played a prominent role during the "Controversies" in Great Britian, will also be presented.

Jung, Adler and Rank will be alluded to tangentially, particularly when their relationship to Freud helped clarify some of the ideological and personality struggles that occurred. The writings of Ferenczi, Abraham, and Jones guide us through the early development of psychoanalytic theory, and introduce us to their important theoretical and political contributions. An examination of the works of Fairbairn and Guntrip will show the full scope of their thinking regarding object-relations theory as a separate theoretical construct from drive theory.

Winnicott stands alone as neither a Freudian or Kleinian, nor a follower of Fairbairn or Guntrip. However, each has influenced him. He was an innovator, a creator, and a critic of drive theory though at times adhering to some drive concepts.

Balint, perhaps a footnote in the history of psychoanalysis has been included because of his close tie to Ferenczi, his sympatica to Freud, some interesting contributions, and a theoretical link between object and drive theory.

Finally, a review of the *Freud-Klein Contoversies—1941–1945* within the Brtish Society is pertinent in order to provide a perspective on the historical conflicts and current issues regarding drive and object theories, and how and in what manner they cast their shadow upon the present.

NOTE

1. I have used the terms "drives" and "instinct" interchangeably throughout this book. Since drives connate somewhat more of an energic quality, it seemed a more preferable term. Also, the word "drive" is closer to everyday usage while "instinct" reflects a more static concept, but is the correct biological term. Freud likewise used the terms intermittenly to connate the same meaning.

Chapter One

Freud

The Progenitor of Object Relations Theory

History is made of major and minor events, some cumulative that result in gradual changes and finally, a new dialectic emerges. Some may present monumental acts seemingly without predecessors, Freud, the visionary and the revolutionary, had his antecedents. Thus, while he was cumulative, a synthesizer of past knowledge and human experience, his insights so revolutionized psychological thinking that history placed him among the monumental.

Whether one carries the torch untarnished, regarding Freud, the man and his theories, or accedes to the onslaught of his critics, it is not possible to discuss most psychological issues without some reference to Freud, albeit positive or negative. Michel Foucault (see Eros, 2004) commented: "Sigmund Freud together with Karl Marx-were founders of discourse, that is, they credited discourse which could have been later challenged, disputed, falsified, but no one can avoid or supersede them" (122).

This study of Freud's theories of the object and object relations is an attempt to assess his contribution to the theoretical and clinical understanding of these concepts and to show that Freud's hypotheses regarding the soma-mind source of drives and their impact on object relationships remains the corner stone of psychoanalytic theory (Blum, 2011).

Unfortunately, subsequent theorists on the "Object" and "Object Relations" (Fairbairn, 1944,1946, 1952; Guntrip, 1961, 1969a; Mitchell and Greenberg, 1983) have either de-emphasized the role of drives or dismissed their importance, and thus, have contributed to much conceptual disarray in the field or as Blum (2011) has indicated "theoretically destabilized and in eager pursuit of new insights" (597). Nonetheless, we must recognize that the

"Object Theorists," by their primary focus on the "object," have intensified our study of its role in mental development, on psychic structure, and have contributed a greater understanding of Object Relations to both drive theory and object theory (Kernberg, 2011).

Unfortunately, little recognition by the object theorists has been accorded to Freud's conceptualizations regarding object, object representation, sexual object, and object relations that were fundamental factors in his postulates regarding psychic development. His concepts on internalization, introjection, and identification could only result from an intrinsic awareness of the infant's relationship to the primary objects in his/her life, and the continuous importance of object relationships throughout life. That Freud viewed drives and objects in a binary relationship has been lost to his adversaries, perhaps due to his more specific focus on the role of the drives.

Interestingly, Aron (1995), a relational psychoanalyst, has taken to task the 'Relationists' but ever so gently. He indicated: "A relational approach does not have to ignore or minimize the importance of childhood sexuality in general or the significance of the Oedipus complex in particular" (197–198). He further stated: "In fact, it is my impression that many analysts working from within the relational traditions have neglected the metaphor of the primal scene; in moving away from a drive-discharge model and in focusing on pre-oedipal phenomena, they have moved away from the sexual and oedipal imagery that dominated psychoanalysis for half a century" (197).

A review of Freud's theories on the object from a thematic and chronological perspective will prove that Freud did not disregard the importance of the object. Rather, he was concerned with the role of the object from early infancy and the processes through which the ego and psychic structure developed. Concepts such as identification, internalization, and the need-gratifying object were formulated quite early in his theories.

A secondary purpose in examining Freud's concepts regarding the significance of the "Object" is not only to correct the current misunderstanding regarding his theories, but also to attempt to understand the underlying rationale for this misreading. Though Freud never wrote a theoretical paper on the object or object relations, a review of his oeuvre from 1895 through 1940 reveals the centricity of objects in his thinking. It is interesting to note that in his posthumous paper, *Project for a Scientific Psychology* (1950[1895]), a work that predates drive theory, Freud's recognition of the role of the object in psychological development was clearly evident. He stated:

> Thus as a result of the experience of satisfaction a facilitation comes about between two mnemic images and the nuclear neurons which are cathected in the state of urgency. No doubt, along with the discharge of satisfaction the Qn flows out of the mnemic images as well. Now, when the state of urgency or wishing reappears, the cathexis will pass over on to the two memories and will

> activate them. Probably the mnemic image of the object will be the first to be affected by the wishful activation (319).

How prophetic is this statement by Freud regarding neurons, facilitations, mnemic images, and memory of the object, in light of current research. (Kandel, 1998; Pankseep, 1998).

There is no question regarding the early onset of the object for the infant both mentally and affectively. The object, the place it assumes in psychic structure and in unconscious conflict, its pivotal role in ego and superego structure, is clearly evident in Freud's major papers, (1915, 1917a,b, 1920a,b, 1923, 1926, 1930, 1937, 1940), in other writings (1910, 1913b), and in his case studies (1905a, 1909a, b, 1918). His writings on identification and internalization and the nature of the transference (1895, 1912, 1914 a, b, 1917a,b, 1923, 1930) signify the importance of the object and object relationships from early infancy, Oedipal, post-Oedipal, and in adult life.

Freud's postulates on drive theory had a direct impact on his theoretical position on the nature of internalization. The dynamic and energic force of the drive helped define the quality of the internalized object. The ebb and flow of libido from ego/self to object reflected both the force of the drives and the nature of the object relationship.

While I will not directly discuss the psychoneuroses or psychopathology, it is important to point out that different writings will stress different components of his theoretical hypothesis. Thus, when Freud considered that the "psychoneurosis are based on sexual instinctual forces. By this I do not merely mean that the energy of the sexual instinct makes a contribution -----. I mean expressly to assert that that contribution is the most important and only source of energy of the neurosis and that in consequence the sexual life of the person in question is expressed . . . " (1905b, 163) he was focusing on a particular theoretical postulate rather than the exclusivity of a particular causal theory. As one reads his case studies, it appears quite evident that the sexual drive has only relevance in relation to the libidinal investment in objects. In the "Rat Man" case (Notes Upon a Case of Obsessional Neurosis, 1909b) the family, particularly his father, was opposed to this relationship and wanted him to marry another woman who was both wealthy and socially well connected. Freud indicated:

> This family plan stirred up in him a conflict as to whether he should remain faithful to the lady he loved in spite of her poverty, or whether he should follow in his father's footsteps and marry the lovely, rich and well–connected girl who had been assigned to him. And he resolved this conflict, which was in fact one between his love and the persisting influence of his father's wishes, by falling ill; or, to put it more correctly, by falling ill he avoided the task of resolving it in real life. . . . The conflict at the root of his illness was in

> essentials a struggle between the persisting influence of his father's wishes and his own amatory predilections (198–200).

In Freud's cases, it is not possible to deny the important role that objects played for him in psychic development, phase maturation, identification, and introjection. Further, the degree by which Freud focused on the "here and now" contradicts the view that the present was immaterial for him. When Freud (1913b) related the number of times a week he saw patients, he indicated that to see patients less than six times a week, at the onset of the analysis, would prohibit dealing with patients' current life events and would do an injustice to the analysis.

Peter Gay (1998) pointed out that Freud was constantly alert to the external world of objects and situations. "The external environment, even if it only occupies the background of most psychoanalytic sessions, is always there." Further, he stated "So intimate and private a conflict as the Oedipus complex is to Freud's mind shaped by outer forces, by experiences in school, at play, through reading" (122). It is important to stress that Freud considered body and mind as interwoven like the threads in a garment, each can only be separated for emphases.

Freud, further, hypothesized that the ego and the superego, a construct of internalized objects, became part of man's phylogenetic inheritance. This is particularly relevant in regard to Freud's numerous claims of an objectless phase (1905b, 1914b) while in other writings he stated that the object and object choice existed almost from the beginning of infancy (1905b, 1916a, 1923). Despite a number of contradictory statements by Freud in regard to onset of object choice, it is clear that the object played a significant role from the beginning of life. The intent is not to disregard the contradictions in Freud's work; yet, it is not possible to have produced such a vast inheritance of intellectual achievement without as Laplanche (1970) has referred to as:

> A certain dialectical approach, entailing an evolution through reversals and crises, mediated by contradictions whose status will not be immediately apparent in any attempt to situate them. Even if, in an interpretative stage, all the contradictions in Freud's thought are perhaps not amenable to the same treatment, not attributable to the same "mechanism" or "agency," they are all deserving of the same "free floating" attention. No doubt, in practice certain contradictions may prove to be relatively "extrinsic" or adventitious, the results of polemic or of hasty formulations; but even in such cases, they cannot be discarded without a certain loss. But it is above all certain large contradictions, traversing Freud's work from one end to the other, which must be interpreted dialectically, either as contradiction of thought—consequently referable to a certain "unspoken" dimension—or as contradictions of the object itself . . . (1).

FREUD AND HISTORY

Freud did not invent the concepts of neurosis or psychosis, nor was he the first to proclaim that unknown regions of the mind, referred to as the subconscious, influenced human behavior. He had his mentors in Warner–Jauregg, Charcot, Janet, somewhat older contemporaries, and even Messmer, one century prior to his findings. As Gay (1988) has indicated, even Thucydides that ancient Greek historian understood the irrationality of the human race, and that "the collective national or racial prejudices or religious passions, compel humans into attitudes and acts that would remain altogether inexplicable if they were studied under the reasonable rubric of raw self interest alone" (121).

Thus, these understandings were not Freud's alone, but it was Freud who with his brilliant insights, became the great systematizer and purveyor of deeper understanding. Breuer, his foremost mentor, called Freud's attention to the "talking cure" and thus, paved the way for his early theories on psychoanalytic treatment. Freud was not the first to focus on sexuality as an important component in psychological development, nor was he the first to recognize the impact of sex in psychic conflict (Kraft-Ebing, 1886; Ellis, 1898; Moll, 1891) all of which is part of history. Yet, Freud succeeded his contemporaries by not only integrating sexuality within the context of the individual's total psychic life, but by formulating a theory of drives that were to become the subject of study for the natural sciences (Panksepp, 1998). Freud positioned the instincts on the border between biology and psychology, a meshing of soma and mind. Soma and mind were united in a dual function affecting mental organization and drive discharge, a biological function and a mental function.

The idea of "lust," well known to nineteenth-century psychology, was metamorphosed into the postulate 'Libido' (Freud, 1895), a mode of psychic energy, as a driving force in the mental economy. Freud viewed Libido as a basic motivating force for individual relationships and social organization (1905b, 1910, 1930). Psychic structure developed from a dynamic confluence of biological imperatives seeking satisfaction and discharge, and ego development accrued by means of the mechanisms of identification and internalization of objects. Freud, the revolutionary thinker by his formulation of instincts as motivating, object, and aim directed, provided an understanding of human behavior that had been compartmentalized by his predecessors and contemporaries.

FREUD'S INSTINCT THEORIES

In this section, I will briefly define Freud's instinct theories.[1] In the next section, I will show the relationship of instincts to objects and the interconnection between them. Freud's early instinct theories anticipated his later evolving concepts of instincts. He initially regarded instincts within the larger corpus of theories that included hunger, mastery, play, and sexuality. The posthumous *Project* written in 1895 has only one reference to instinct, and that is, "Trieb," wherein, he indicated: "we know it by the power of the will as a derivative of the instincts" (317). He made no great claim for the role of sexuality except as it became increasingly evident that repression of sexual desires determined much of neurotic symptomatology. The early papers on Hysteria (1893–1895) concerned the mechanism of repression of unacceptable ideas and its impact on mental functions. Concepts of discharge as a means of dealing with repression and psychic damming predominated in his writings and evidenced the influence on him by the dominant theorists of his age, Fechner, Meynert, and Darwin (Gay, 1998; Kurzweil, 1998). Freud's main theses focused on the organism's need for homeostatic equilibrium, a concept that later evolved into the pleasure–unpleasure principle.

By 1905, in the *Three Essays*, Freud developed a more specific and unified instinct theory that conflated mental and biologic processes.[2] He formulated a two instinct theory, the ego instincts and the sexual instincts that largely determined the organization and character of psychic development and conflict. The ego instincts were defined by their self-preservative quality while the sexual instincts strove for both procreation of the species and individual gratification. It is in regard to the sexual instincts that Freud referred to the "sexual object," the object that is the vehicle through which procreation and personal pleasure is achieved. In a subsequent section, I will elaborate on Freud's concept of the "sexual object" and the seeming contradiction between the nature of the "sexual object" and the object. The question remains whether this contradiction is more apparent than real?

The second instinct theory emerged in the 1920 paper *Beyond the Pleasure Principle*. Here Freud unified the ego instincts with the sexual instincts under one rubric, Eros, and proposed the second drive theory as the Death Instinct, Thanatos. Psychic conflict developed from the conflicting motives of Eros, which is the life force, a binding drive, and Thanatos, a drive to death, to undue life, to reduce life to its former inorganic state, a state of nirvana.

Aggression as a derivative of Thanatos stands independently of libidinal frustration, and henceforth, is on equal footing with the sexual drive as a component in molding psychic development. Fusion and binding of the two drives are processes in developing defense mechanisms and control of discharge. Perhaps, what is most interesting is that Freud did not give aggression a fully independent status but, rather, aligned it with the death drive and preferred to regard aggression as a derivative of Thanatos. He further, distanced himself from Adler who had earlier postulated the aggressive drive, though Adler's theory became increasingly removed from a biological concept of instincts. Many analysts have disagreed with Freud's concept of the "Death Drive" (Jones, 1935; Fenichel, 1953a,b; Hartmann, Kris, and Loewenstein, 1953; Stone, 1971) preferring either the concept of an aggressive drive or viewing aggression as reactive to libidinal frustration.

FREUD'S OBJECT THEORIES

Freud's concepts of the "object," object relationships, the internalization of the object and identification permeate all of his principle writings. Drives and object were viewed as a confluence, each meriting importance at various developmental stages. Yet, the question as to why he did not write even one monograph on the "Object" as an independent focus has no answer. The assumption could be made, ala his critics, Mitchell and Greenberg (1983), that he regarded object relations as almost irrelevant or minor causative factors in psychic development and in mental conflict. Though, they recognized that the concept of object relations "originated as an inherent part of Freud's drive theory," it was felt that the object played a subsidiary role. They proffered that the problem for psychoanalysis has been the continual quest for the role of object relations into theory. "This is a result of Freud's original drive theory that takes the discharge of psychic energy as its fundamental conceptual building block, assigning to relations with others a statue which is neither central nor immediately apparent" (379). Yet, as previously indicated, Freud's major writings have repeated references to the centricity of the object in psychic structure and psychic conflict. To hypothesize, it is possible to[3] posit that the role of the object for Freud was a self-evident truism, and that a libido theory without an inherent relationship to the object could serve only as a partial explanation of psychic development. Therefore, the role of the object was an implicit assumption, and did not require a more detailed explication.

As early as the *Project* (1950[1895]), Freud had already evolved a theory of the object's role in his attempts to find a psycho-neurological basis for mental functioning and psychic structure. Freud indicated that the object in its role as satisfier of the instincts, such as, hunger, becomes immediately connected to drive discharge and is, therefore, an integral component of the quality and the aim of discharge. The object representation is first preceded by a "thing" presentation that results in the establishment of a mnemic image of the object. The libidinal investment in the "thing" presentation derives from the infant relationship to the nurturing object, which established a permanent mnemic image of the object. These early object relationships define drive states not simply by quantitative factors but, importantly, determine qualitative aspects of the object relationship.

Thus, following Freud's thinking, discharge of drive states from early infancy cannot be treated as objectless drive states, but are interwoven with the nature of object satisfaction. Freud further indicated that "qualities are linked with perception," and desire for the object as well as desire for satisfaction could therefore be viewed as the multifaceted aim of the instincts. Though Freud was focusing on the development of wish, perception, thought, and cognition, underlying these concepts was the mode by which the object was established as a mnemic image, as a presentation, and was internalized as a stable object representation.

Discharge as drive releasing and tension reduction, a principle concept in Freud's economic theories, was intimately connected to both the internal and external object. Therefore, the aim, whose goal was initially gratification through release of tension, that is, discharge, was itself modified in connection with the particular object of gratification. Aim and object exists as two separate entities, the former in reference to function and the latter as part of psychic structure. It is equally valid to assume that object and aim are the two inter-connecting forces operative in the mode of libidinal strivings and discharge.

Further, Freud stated that in regard to objects "an object *like this* was simultaneously the (subject's) first satisfying object, and further his first hostile object as well as his sole helping power . . . " (*Project*, 331). The object, functioning as the primary agent for gratification, becomes the means by which the subject becomes a cognizant human being. He also indicated that:

> At first, the human organism is incapable of bringing about specific actions. It takes: place by extraneous help, when attention of an experienced person is drawn to the child's state by discharge along the path of internal change. In this way this path of discharge acquires a secondary function of the highest importance, that of *communication*, and the initial helplessness of human beings is the *primal source* of all moral motives (318).

This concept of the mode by which the object is established in psychic structure almost from birth was again referred to in *Inhibition, Symptoms and Anxiety* (1926), some thirty-one years later. In Freud's discussion of the early precipitates of anxiety, the birth trauma, he stated:

> We cannot possibly suppose that the fetus has any sort of knowledge of its life being destroyed. It can only be aware of some vast disturbance in the economy of its narcissistic libido. Large sums of excitation crowd in upon it, giving rise to new kinds of feelings of unpleasure, and some organs acquire an increased

cathexis, thus foreshadowing the object—cathexis which will soon set in (135).

FREUD'S SEXUAL OBJECT

Freud's reference to the object as a "sexual object" or a "drive object" has led to much controversy even for the classically oriented analysts. Compton, an exponent of classical theory (1981, 1983a,b, 1985, 1986) indicated that Freud's "drive-directed object," or "sexual object" appears to undermine or at least diminish the importance that he gave to the object and object choice prior to the Oedipal phase.

Though, Freud repeatedly interchanged the terms sexual object and the object, we have to question what his frame of reference was. Was the reference to different, isolated object representations or did these terms, that is, sexual object and object, refer to qualitatively different aspects of the same object in regard to a variety of developmental functions and aims? The same object may simultaneously be the subject of various unconscious fantasies and mnemic representations at different developmental phases and in various disguises. Furthermore, the developmental sequence of object relationships, and the maturation of libidinal phases results in differentiated qualities of the same object representation. Different drive investment in the object, that is, aggression, libido, and component instincts determine the specific subjective affect and memory of the object at a particular moment (Model, 1990). Therefore, the suggestion is put forth, that Freud regarded "sexual object" and "object" as initially identical. The sexual object assumes a qualitatively different characteristic in puberty and in adult life in the search for a different, non-incestuous object.

Historically, the term "sexual object" first appeared in *The Project* (1895). Freud's concept of the "sexual object" and the "object" are best understood from a contextual reading. The usage tends to reflect a particular meaning defined by the relationship between subject and object. Freud at various times referred to the object that provided "nourishment" as a "sexual object" (1895). This statement was as surprising as it was prescient for later theories for at this period, his theories on infantile sexuality and the sexual instincts had not been formulated.

Strachey, in his Introduction to (1950[1895]) pointed out that in his (Freud's) early work there is a major difference from his later theories, "all emphasis in the picture here is upon the environment's impact upon the organism and the organism's reaction to it." The main interest is upon the defensive operations and their mechanisms. Further, he indicated that it is in *The Project* that we can find a "foretaste" of the structural ego that formally emerges in *The Ego and the Id* (1923). "Internal forces are scarcely more than secondary reactions to external ones." The ego instincts and sexual instincts have not yet evolved in his thinking and the Id, in fact, is still to be postulated (291–292).

In the *Three Essays on Sexuality* (1905b), Freud again uses the term "sexual object." This has been interpreted to mean an object that serves the sexual drive in the most concrete sense of the word. To be a sexual object seems to connote a meaning close to orgiastic functions or physical discharge and, therefore, appears to predicate an object devoid of emotional attachment. Freud did not regard the sexual drive as a simple action of discharge but, also, as has been indicated, as a mode for establishing object relationships. It serves the purpose of survival of the species and simultaneously provides the emotional basis for human relationships. Libido was viewed as a force that functioned as a unifier of individual and group processes (Freud, 1920b).

The relationship between the instincts and the object, and the so-called "sexual object," was essential to his metapsychological premise, in particular, to the genetic factor. True, Freud is quite categorical in his thinking that though the internalized object underlies the basic fabric of psychic structure, the compelling and motivating force in psychic development derives from the clamor of the instincts for satisfaction. It is in this sense that Freud spoke of a "sexual object," that is, an object whose purpose is to gratify the instincts. Satisfaction, in the context of Freud's usage, arises from biological needs that demand relief. Eventually, we would have to consider whether psychological and emotional needs take precedence over biology or at least are equal in demand for satisfaction.

The mode or aim of discharge is defined by two sources, the erotogenic zones, determined by maturation, and by the specific response from the object. The central nervous system, the neurological base of emotional response, and cognition are functionally dependent on the drives and the object for its development as an organic structure, that is, the development of the mind. Though, Freud considered the aim of the sexual drive as that of discharge and the "sexual object" as the source and aim of satisfaction, it is clear from his writings that this same sexual object is transformed into an object of both love and hate through the process of identification, internalization, sublimation, and frustration. Furthermore, we consider that this process occurs at every developmental stage. Sexual phases influence the characteristics of the internalized object that in turn modifies the drives.

Another misconception has centered on Freud's statement regarding the variability of the "sexual object." This has also provided the opponents of drive theory with ammunition to assert that the role of the object in psychic development was of minor importance (Greenberg and Mitchell, 1983). Granted, evidence for this criticism can be found in *Group Psychology and the Analysis of the Ego* (1921) and *The Ego and the Id* (1923). For example, Freud (1923) indicated that "It is found in erotic cathexis where a peculiar indifference in regard to the object displays itself; and it is especially evident in the transferences arising in analysis that develop inevitably irrespective of the persons who are their object" (4). Freud (1923) regarded this capacity to displace objects as a product of sublimation, a means of loosening the erotic cathexis from the pre-oedipal object, and the incestuous object of the Oedipal phase. He indicated there could be a loosening of object ties when the object was an erotic object and, as a sexual object, it is displaceable. Yet, there can be no question that Freud considered that a primary object is established and maintained throughout life. Freud (1923, 1926) repeatedly stated that in the course of our search for an object we are always looking to refind an old object, the object of our earliest infancy.

What then, can we conclude regarding Freud's ad hoc usage of "sexual object" and "object"? Is it similar to his usage of ego and self, each term employing a similar referent and used interchangeably? Since Freud regarded the first object as a libidinal object and the relationship to the object as libidinal, is it fair to assume that he regarded the quality of the libidinal investment in the primary object as subject to change and modification through the mental processes of sublimation, narcissism, identification, defense, and aim? Therefore, Freud saw no contradiction in his intermittent use of both the "sexual object" and the "object."

In *Inhibitions, Symptoms and Anxiety* (1926), Freud no longer made the distinction between the "sexual object" and the "object." Freud established a hierarchy of dangerous situations, each of which reflected the centricity of the object and the danger that accrued from loss of the object. The first of these dangers arose from the threat of loss of the need-gratifying object, an object that is closest to the evolution of the ego's differentiation from the Id; and that this phase would appear to be the least likely one to reflect a "sexual object." Yet, it is precisely to this phase (1895, 1905) that Freud gave the nomenclature, a "sexual object," an object that is cathected with libido, in spite of the more likely phase, the Oedipal stage in which genital sexuality is pronounced. The danger of loss reflects qualitatively different affective relationships to the object at various developmental phases. Theses affective derivatives are reflective of quantitative as well as qualitative factors, such as love and hate that are inherent in the instincts. Other derivatives of sexuality refer to affects such as friendship, affection, kindness, sympathy, and empathy. The point is that Freud considered all objects as invested with libido, regardless of the vicissitudes that sexuality has undergone in aim and function. This paper reflected Freud's recognition of the singular importance of the object, and the dangers inherent in loss of the object.

In his paper *The Dynamics of Transference* (1912), Freud distinguished between the erotic desires for the analyst and an affectionate current, both of which stem from sexual libido. "Originally," he stated," we knew only sexual objects; and psychoanalysis shows us that people who in our real life are merely admired or respected may still be sexual objects for our unconscious" (105).

Thus, the complexity of meaning regarding the "sexual object" lies in the multitude of meanings that have accrued in the course of psychic development and in civilization's cultural development. Eroticism, love, and sex are the many aspects of the human emotion; they require a contextual understanding in relation to real life, the nature of object relationships, the character traits of the individual, specific needs, dependency, internalizations, and sublimation. The list is in all probability longer as to what differentiates love from sex and sexual love. Therefore, Freud's apparent division between a "sexual object" and a "love object" would appear to be a matter of emphasis at a particular point in his thinking and a less than exact precision in his writings. Our reading regarding the "object" and the "sexual object" should reflect the complexity of differentiated functions of the internal object, and the multitudinous needs and desires of the subject in relation to the object.

OBJECT CHOICE

The concept of the Drive Object (Compton, 1985), or the Sexual Object, as already discussed in the above paragraph, has created a good deal of misunderstanding regarding Freud's ideas on the "object," and object choice. In the *Three Essays on the Theory of Sexuality* (1905b), Freud made a number of statements that on the surface would seem to corroborate perceptions that Freud conceived of an early objectless phase and that object choice was established only at the Oedipal phase (Compton, 1985). For example, Freud stated that "The sexual instinct is not unified and is at first without an object, and the early efflorescence of infantile sexual life gives rise to the "choice of an object," that occurred around the ages of "2–5" (234) originating in the phallic-oedipal phase. Yet, a closer reading of those statements indicating that object choice was established in the phallic-oedipal phase are contradicted by Freud's frequent references to the choice of the object and the attachment to the object (1915, 1950) in early infancy.

His ideas on love (1905b) for the mother in the oral phase and subsequent statements that the finding of an object is in essence a re-finding of the object is a clear indication that object choice began in early infancy. In *Civilization and Its Discontents* (1930), he indicated that object choice and identification were parallel processes. Yet, he also, equivocated as to which process was the earlier, again referring to the infant phase. In his discussion of the prototype of the pubertal object, he stated that it is the mother who succors the infant at her breast and the "preparations for finding the object at puberty" were made from the earliest childhood experiences. He further indicated: "The subordination of all the other sources of sexual excitation under the primacy of the genital zones and the process of finding an object . . . are already adumbrated in childhood" (1905b, 222). Freud's views on the nature or inherent qualities that motivated selection of a love object was rooted in earliest infancy, indeed almost from the beginning of life. He referred to two methods that influence the quality of the object choice. One was determined by the anaclitic or attachment relationship of infancy and the second one reflected a narcissistic object choice (1916b, 1917).

Perhaps, one can question the exact nature of identification as either an end result of a psychic process, that is, as a noun, or as a verb, to act to identify. Does identification require a relationship to an object, thus to presume action, to take in, to incorporate as a "mirror state" (Freud, 1917) or is the process essentially a representation of the object, therefore an identification? We could presume that both processes occur almost simultaneously, with the object representation a more delayed step based on psychic development (Sandler and Rosenblatt, 1962). Jacobson (1964) raised similar questions regarding the difference between self and self-representations, and the manner by which they were structured. Her conclusions were rather ambiguous, and one is left with the sense that they belong to similar processes and internalized states.

Again, we are met with another group of contradictions when we examine various aspects of Freud's theories on autoerotism and narcissism regarding timing of object representation and object choice. Autoerotism and narcissism (1914b) functionally have similar relationships to the object or more precisely, lack of relationship. Freud indicated that initially the primary narcissistic state is objectless as is the autoerotic phase. In these states, the ego has no need of the external world. He further stated that the "auto-erotic instincts, however are there from the very first; so there must be something added to auto-eroticism—a new psychical action to bring about narcissism" (77). This statement is indeed bewildering for Freud had previously claimed that the object is invested with libido from the very beginning of life and is set down in the mind as an mnemic presentation. Further, as has been indicated in the preceding paragraph, Freud (1905b, 1930) stated that object choice and identification are almost concurrent processes that begin at the onset of infant life. The conundrum may best explained by means of the relative investment of libido in the object and the self. The narcissistic state is never a pure state of objectless. Narcissism, from an energic perspective, implies distribution of libido but libido, that has been transformed from a direct self-investment to sexuality and also love for the object.

The issue of sexual gratification in reference to feeding appears as an oxymoron. How are we to equate sexuality with food and survival? For Freud affect states and survival mechanisms are equated with the nature of sexuality. This question is one of a psychological state reflecting an affective relationship between self and object. These are issues of both a quantitative distribution of libido and a qualitative factor. To conceive of love as a static affective state is contrary to empirical evidence. Love is subject to development, parallel with psychosexual development. It implies the qualities of empathy and identification and the nature of the object relationship. Thus, within this conceptual framework, narcissism, though presented in energic terms, is primarily defined by the quality of libidinal investment in the self and in the object (Freud, 1914b, 1923). Freud's ideas regarding qualitative and quantitative considerations had been outlined in his distinction between primary and secondary narcissism (1914b), and in previous references to qualitative and quantitative factors in *The Project* (1950).

In regard to autoeroticism, we are faced with the same issue of a phase of development that Freud (1914b) indicated was objectless. Since our textual readings of Freud have shown that he considered that object relations and object choice occur very early in psychic development, how are we to understand this meaning of autoerotism especially since he indicated that it preceded narcissism? Is it possible to assume that from the perspective of a direct sexual gratification, the infant due to his/her motoric and cognitive development developed the capacity to self-gratify? This was thus the origin of the first masturbatory acts that became fully integrated in the later genital phase. Masturbatory acts or self-gratification do not, ipso facto, require an external object. In this act, the nascent object representation or identificatory object may remain in a quiescent, minimally cathected, libidinal state. While this explanation may appear as a logical answer to Freud's placement of autoerotism as the first state in libidinal development, it does not fully answer the issues posed by Freud in *On Narcissism* whether autoerotism relates to the sexual libido or to ego libido (Laplanche, 2015). We are left here with some confusion in Freud's thinking since he never fully clarified his thinking in regard to the nature of ego libido, object libido, and narcissistic libido. We may even add to the list homosexual libido. Therefore, how to understand these qualifying appellations since he considered that ego libido and object libido were "reducible to biology," that is, an economic state, and not a qualitative state?

In the attempt to unify Freud's theories, it is not possible to absolve him from leaving an inheritance of contradictions. Freud did state that it was at the Oedipal phase that object choice was established (1905b). Thus, the proposal that Freud was focusing on the various qualities of the internalized object according to different drive states, that is, oral, anal, and phallic/genital, that also reflected successive maturational phases has validity. Further, it is suggested that he was concerned with the characteristics of specific periods imprinted by zonal phases that give particular definition to the nature and character of the ego and the internal object representation. Thus, when he was discussing object choice at the Oedipal phase it is probable to assume that he was referring to the object that could serve the re-productive aspect of the sexual drive and not the qualitative, emotional connection to the object, an object choice that had been established in infancy. Given the history of his writings on love and identification, the likely contention is that he was attempting to establish a developmental and hierarchical sequence involved in object choice. Thus, object choice at the Oedipal phase was concerned more with the specific sexual role of the object and the sexual identification of the subject.

From the full canon of Freud's writings, the evidence does not substantiate the claim that object choice was established only at the Oedipal phase. Yet, it is not possible to avoid the different contradictory statements regarding the development and timing of internalization, object relationships, and object choice. Perhaps, it is possible to conclude that various concepts were approached in isolation from other concepts and only by a reading of the total oeuvre can one ascertain Freud's fundamental thinking.

GENERAL WRITINGS—REFERENCE TO EGO/SELF, IDENTIFICATION, INTERNALIZATION, AND STRUCTURE

Freud's major sociological treatises, *Totem and Taboo* (1913a), *Group Psychology and the Analysis of the Ego* (1921), *The Future of an Illusion* (1927), and *Civilization and Its Discontents* (1930), are replete with references to the role of the object as central to man's emotional and social development. His concepts regarding identification, internalization, and incorporation derive from drive investment in objects, a process that has inception from birth. The nature of empathy, an affect derived from identification, is indicative of the mutual relation between the object and the ego (1921, 110). In *Totem and Taboo* (1913a), Freud stated that the "root of religion is the longing for the father" (148) and he viewed neurosis as asocial structures. He commented: "To turn away from reality is to turn away from the community of man" (148). In *Group Psychology and the Analysis of the Ego* (1921), Freud also posited, "Identification is known to psychoanalysis as the earliest expression of an emotional tie with another person" (105). He stressed that in the individual's mental life "Someone else is invariably involved, as a model, as an object, as a helper, and as an opponent; and so from the very first individual psychology is at the same time social psychology." (69).

The papers on *Narcissism* (1914b), *Instincts and their Vicissitudes* (1915b), and *Mourning and Melancholia* (1917) were directly focused on the specific role of the object, the self, and the ego-ideal. The interdependence of love and identification led Freud to consider a more detailed concept of the self and the object relationship. In these papers, an increased concern with the development of the self-structure and the role of internalization emerged. Where formerly these concepts were stated in rather broad outline, Freud increasingly refined the dynamic process whereby libido invested in self and in object resulted in psychic structure. Identification was increasingly viewed as both a process and a defense mechanism (1905a[1901]; 1917a[1915]) and foreshadowed his seminal paper *The Ego and the Id* (1923).

Freud gave equal weight to the qualitative relationship of self and object as he did to the role of instinctual vicissitudes as the bases of psychic structure. The ego as a specific agency of the mind had been for Freud a self-evident postulate (1895, 1900). However, increasingly in his writings, the gradations in ego functions led to the structural theory. Freud (1915b) stated that as objects present themselves as sources of pleasure, they are taken into the ego, they are "introjected," but when they become sources of unpleasure they are "expelled." Further, he stated: "in so far as the ego is auto-erotic it has no need of the external world, but as a consequence of experience undergone by the instinct of self preservation, it acquired objects from the world" (135). The object is acquired in the stage of "primary narcissism," and the object cathexis is established from the experiences of satisfaction in the dyadic relationship.

The paper on *Mourning and Melancholia* (1917) elaborated on the mechanism of introjection, albeit, the focus was on the pathological aspects. Yet, of the three metapsychological papers (1914b; 1915; 1917) this was the most central to his development of the structural theory (Ogden, 2002), and it is in this paper that the concept of the ego as a precipitate of abandoned object cathexes was most clearly formulated. This paper indicated that Freud began to recognize that the process of internalization required further exploration and defining. In his earlier paper "On Narcissism" (1914b), Freud had also been interested in the interaction between the ego or self (these were often used interchangeably) and object. Concepts of introjection of the object, the relationship between identification and object love, and the differentiation of the two were not dealt with until *Group Psychology and the Analysis of the Ego* (1921) and *The Ego and the Id* (1923). Though already in *Mourning and Melancholia* (1917) he had already begun consideration of the relationship between the ego and the object and the role of identification as "a preliminary stage of object choice" (249), he then proceeded to elaborate on pathological states where the object either for external reasons or compelling internal conflicts was abandoned. He noted that the "shadow of the object" falls upon the ego and "if the love for the object cannot be relinquished though the object itself is given up then this love takes refuge in "narcissistic identification" (251). He also indicated that the "Melancholic's erotic cathexis in regard to his object has undergone a double vicissitude, part of it has regressed to identification, but, the other part, under the influence of the conflict due to ambivalence, has been carried back to the stage of sadism that is nearer to the conflict" (251–252).

The concept of identification as a defense appeared as a new thought, though there is historical precedence in the Dora case (1905a, *Fragment of an Analysis of a Case of Hysteria*). Perhaps the most crucial element in this paper was the recognition of the manner by which a hated object is internalized and incorporated into the patient's ego. Freud emphasized the dominance of the object in human development and the ego's inability to flourish without objects, even a hated one. The self-attacks in melancholia are essentially attacks against the hated object. The character of the incorporated object and the self-subject are further defined by psychosexual developmental stages. This interpolation of drive and object added depth to the nature of the object and sexuality in psychic life.

This paper (1917), represented a major theoretical advance in Freud's writings for attention was now shifted to the specific processes of internalization within the ego and a somewhat different structural relationship to the ego ideal. Prior to this, the ego and the ego instincts were not the primary focus of Freud's work. Freud regarded the duality of the instincts, that is, the conflict between the ego instincts and the sexual instinct, and the resultant defense mechanisms, as the essential component for the development of the "nervous system," the mental structure, and even social organization.

It was inevitable that in the evolution of Freud's theories, based as they were on clinical data, that he would be confronted with the evolving role of the object in the formation of ego structure. As Freud developed his theories on psychic structure, the role of the object based on clinical findings became more integrated into his structural conceptualization.

The evolution of Freud's theoretical data on the ego, the ego ideal, and structural considerations culminated in *The Ego and the Id* (1923). The first object cathexes that form the ego are the very same objects that also structure the superego. Freud (1923) posited that both agencies are constructed on the basis of the identifications "made in the earliest childhood" (31), and from the abandoned object cathexis. He further added, "this is not in the first instance the consequence or outcome of an object cathexis; it is a direct and immediate identification and takes place earlier than the object cathexis" (31). Future object choices particularly those belonging to the "first sexual period" and those early relationships to the "father and the mother seem normally to find their outcome in an identification of this kind, and reinforce the primary one" (31). From this perspective of Freud, it would appear that the superego has a very early inception for it derives from the "first choices of the Id" (46). Indeed, Freud indicated that it is the superego that lends its hand to the suppression of the Oedipus complex. The superego is not only structured by the first objects of identification, but is later modified by the identificatory object of the Oedipus complex.

That Freud did not elaborate on the introjected object and the effect that disparate, contradictory object identifications have on the psychic structure in a theoretical treatise, does not take away from his recognition of the object's role in psychic development. Certainly this issue emerged in his case studies. There can be no question that he clearly recognized the implication of varying identifications and object cathexes in symptom formation and pathological development. Further, the structure of the psychic apparatus was not simply a direct derivative of the internalized objects.

In discussion on the superego formation, he indicated that the superego was not only a "residue of the earliest object choices of the Id, it represented an energetic reaction formation against these choices" (39). From these readings, the external object is always to some degree, modified, contaminated, or restructured by some internal force. That force is a derivative of the drives. The internalized object is an object that does not simply replicate the external object but that the object representation undergoes some qualitative change in the internalization due to the impact of the drives.

In the above discussion, I have attempted to follow the theoretical process by which Freud was led to his concepts of the tripartite structure of the mind. Internalization of objects was primary to the creation of psychic structure, plus, a discrete body of mental functions that comprise self and assimilated object representations. The self is a composite of internalizations, interfused with drives, evolving in accordance with psychosexual phases, a substrate of biology and psychology.

Freud's metapsychological schema reflected an uncompromising recognition of the nature and role of the object in mental development. The idea of "abandoned object cathexis," while suggestive of relinquishment of the object, refers only to that process by which the object is internalized and assimilated within the ego, that is, self and object representations. Even the Id, the "water shed of the drives," is considered by Freud as a phylogenetic repository of man's personal and social history, the values, idealizations, and characteristics of people and civilization. It is not possible to address issues of ego and superego pathology or normality without understanding the manner by which object relations have affected these structures. In particular, the demands and requirements of the family, the parental objects, the libidinal and aggressive desires toward those objects, and the reaction formations against the objects of identification (*The Ego and the Id*, 1923). The interaction between drive and object, object and structure, and drive is evidenced in all of Freud's thinking.

CONCLUSION

This review of Freud's thinking has aimed to present an accurate picture of the role of the object and to refute the idea that he relegated the object to the realm of lèse majesté. The object from his initial work was unquestionably the primary conduit through which the mechanisms of internalization, identification, and representation were established. By hypothesizing a phylogenetic origin to the Id and superego, Freud further acknowledged the object's role as a historical antecedent in psychological structure. Though the vicissitudes of the internalized object representations were not a central focus in his writings, Freud certainly exhumed the role of the object from the ashes of degeneracy and constitutional heredity, prominent theories of his time, regarding the psychoneurosis (Kraft-Ebing, 1886). That Freud regarded the instincts as the primary motivating force in mental development and causative factors in the psychoneurosis in no way lessoned the role of the object as a concurrent force in psychic structure. The interdependent role of both drive and object is at the essence of Freud's metapsychology.

The question arises as to why Freud's object theories have been negated or dismissed as negligible. Certainly they have provided a source for future investigation and have paved the road for deeper understandings. Greenberg and Mitchell (1983), both Interpersonal analysts, had recognized this trend to demonize the drives. They stated that in order to deal with the centricity of object relations in psychic structure, theorists have either derived "relations with others as derivative of the drives, and thus, of secondary importance or have completely remolded theory to replace a drive theory model with an object relations model" (3).

The failure of the early object theorists, Fairbairn (1952) and Guntrip (1961) to recognize Freud as their most significant predecessor or, in so minimizing his contribution to theories of object relations, provided the base line for the extinction of drive theory in clinical work. Unfortunately, the negation of drives has resulted in a restructured theory of psychic development. The emphasis has shifted to the manifest experience with the object and under-values the impact of drives, defense, ego structure (Rangel, 2002), and most importantly, the dynamic unconscious (Glover, 1937; Shapiro, 1990).

NOTES

1. The question of how Freud conceived of instincts is indeed challenging. Strachey (1950) raised the issue of contradictions in Freud's characterization of "instincts as a frontier concept," and Laplanche and Pontalis (1973) also indicated some contradictions with his formulation. Wakefield (1990), in two papers on Freud and his instinct theories, presented a very different evaluation and provided an important point of clarity.

While the issues regarding the nature of instincts raises more questions than can be answered by our current state of psychological, neurological, and biological knowledge, still the issue has been addressed from many perspectives. Loewald (1978) differed from Freud's basic concepts. He felt there was a duality in his concepts, and indicated that Freud places the instincts on the border between soma and psyche, thus emphasizing the biological root of the instinct as an internal force. Yet, in *Instincts and Their Vicissitudes* (1915), Loewald considered that Freud referred to instincts as "the mental representative of organismic stimuli," stressing the mental. It is this seeming contradiction and Freud's preference for the biological focus that Loewald (1951, 1978) suggested that Freud's model is a closed system.

In Loewald's (1980) conceptualization "psychic representative" indicated the mental, "the psychological factor of the drives, the idea (vorstellung), and therefore instinct falls within the purview of the psychological." Loewald defined instinct as a "mental force or stimulus and may be described as the most primitive element unit of motivation" (19). Further, he would say that the object does not become "assigned to the instinct (understood as psychic force) but contributes crucially to the organization of instincts qua instincts, just as instinctual forces crucially contribute to the organization of objects qua objects" (130).

Brenner (1982) indicated that drives "are psychological phenomena." Libido and aggression, derive from the functioning of the brain, they "are driving forces that motivate mental activity" (24). The difference between Loewald and Brenner lie in their theoretical positions regarding the source of the drives. Loewald conceived of the mother-child dyad as the basic source of drive stimulus and its organizing factor while Brenner considered the drives as mental energy unrelated to physical energy.

2. I am using the term "source" differently from Freud's delineation of source. He defined the source of the drives as emanating from erotogenic zones. I am using the term in a psychological sense only and in no way negate his delineation in the *Three Essays* of our understanding of the sexual drive by its object, aim, and source.

3. It is beyond the purview of this book to discuss Freud's theories of instinct as separate from their interchange with object formation and function, but it is suggested that one read Wakefield (1990).

Chapter Two

Freud's Case Studies

The Hidden Object

To present Freud's case studies may appear as a redundancy given the amount of literature devoted to them (Kanzer and Glenn, 1980; Gardiner, 1970; Deutsch, F., 1957). Yet what better way to show the explicit role of the object in his thinking than to review actual case material. To read Freud's cases presents one with not only the acuity of his insights and his skill, but astonishingly, his personal engagement with the patient. His work flies against the accusations of classical analysis as a one-dimension treatment process with the analyst as sole arbiter of the treatment.

Freud engaged with his patients in a teaching process by providing understanding and knowledge regarding the unconscious, the defenses used, and how and why symptoms are formed. This method is both didactic, emotionally laden, and object related. The patient becomes a partner in the work, a knowledgeable person whose ideas matter. Isakower (1936) claimed that the analytic method is essentially a two-person model (see Reiser, 1985), and this is how Freud functioned in the analytic situation. Further, Freud (1940) indicated that analysis works by working through the transference and resistance, using suggestion, teaching, and providing insight. Let us recall that it was Freud who first gave recognition to the concept of countertransference.

Anna Freud (1971), in a foreword to *The Wolf-Man by the Wolf-Man* (Gardiner, 1971), indicated that there was a "dearth of publications in a specific direction: that of complete and adequately documented case studies." As a result the teaching institutes have relied heavily on the studies by Freud ("Little Hans," "Dora," "The Rat Man," "The Wolf-Man," "Schreiber," and "Anna O.") all of which have enriched our knowledge of the neurosis and the psychosis. She further indicated:

> On the other hand the success in summarizing, condensing, selecting, and synthesizing material, which made these stories so eminently readable, also had some unsuspected results. The very familiarity which analysts began to feel with these patients aroused the temptation to deal with them in their imagination as if they were their own patients, to wish to know everything about them, to test the interpretations given, to probe beyond the conclusions drawn, and where ever possible to reconstitute once more the original data from which the author's abstractions had been made (x).

Regrettably, the book, *Freud and His Patients* (edited by Kanzer and Glenn 1980), an excellent compendium of theorists, must be accused of this very fact. No one can really quarrel with the writers' astute clinical and theoretical observations except to note that their evaluations unfairly judge Freud's treatment methods, his conclusions that arise from the very beginnings of psychoanalytic treatment, and theory. To blame the originator for what he didn't do or know demands too much perfection. To be laudatory does not result in syncopathy and to be unnecessarily critical is no great feat. Though Scharfman (1980) lauds Freud, he also echoes the general criticism regarding Freud's failure to view Dora as an adolescent. Other critiques involve issues regarding his failure to recognize Dora's negative transference and, at times, extending the parameters of psychoanalysis in other cases.

In discussing Freud's case studies of "Little Hans," "Dora," "The Rat Man," and "The Wolf-Man," it is not easy to avoid Anna Freud's characterization of subsequent analysts who have attempted to re-analyze the cases and to make them their own. It is hoped that this author does not succumb to the same temptation.

LITTLE HANS:
THE ANALYSIS OF A PHOBIA IN A FIVE-YEAR-OLD-BOY

Criticism has been leveled at Freud for either his neglect or omission in the treatment of Little Hans of any discussion or reference to the character of the mother, her behavior with her children, her own neurosis and, in particular, her treatment of Hanna, Hans's younger sister (Blum, 2007; Chusid, 2007; Wakefield, 2007). John Munder Ross (2007) stated that Frau Graf's (the mother) "sexual seduction and emotional manipulation of her son, which acerbated his-age-expectable castration and separation anxiety, and her beating of her infant daughter . . . " were the more important causal aspects of his phobia and fears. He further indicated that Hans's symptoms can "therefore be deconstructed not only as the expression of his Oedipal fantasy, but as a communication of the traumatic abuse in the home" (779–780). Blum (2007) accentuated the aspect of pre-oedipal trauma, the angry, violent mother who beat his sister, who preferred Hans and overly eroticized their relationship. It was the traumatic environment for Hans that was the primary source of his phobia. Inherent in these critiques of Freud's treatment is a criticism that he overlooked the destructive behavior in the mother and the role of trauma that were the primary causes in Hans's symptomatology and not the oedipal conflicts.

When Freud gave up his initial theory that actual seduction was at the root of all neurotic symptoms, he introduced the concept of psychic trauma. What exactly did Freud mean by this? Was he emphasizing an economic determinant, asserting that the ego could only handle a certain level of excitation, thus referring to sexual and aggressive stimulation and omitting any factors that dealt with object relationships? Did he also ignore the role of the ego and its inherent strength or weakness in mastering stimuli and the basic impact of the object on ego development? Thus, did his economic theories omit the role of genetic factors (Hartmann, 1939) on ego development, and fail to give weight to possible object loss on ego development? I raise these questions, for I believe that they underlie much of the criticisms that have been directed against Freud, particularly, in relation to his case studies.

It is especially salient that Jennifer Stuart (2007), in her commentary on the case of Little Hans, seemed to ask for more tolerance and indicated that "More than a century has passed since Freud first met Olga Graf. . . . Do a few more morsels of information give us the warrant to question Freud's original observations and conclusions?" It would appear that what we may add to the interpretations or stressing the pre-oedipal (Wakefield, 2007) factors does not take away from the thorough and minute attention to the details of Little Hans's associations and material that eventually leads us to the core of his phobia. To blame is to deny how future knowledge had been built on a cornerstone of Freud's investigations and thus, set the course for further exploration.

Can we accuse Einstein for omissions in his "theories on relativity," Hippocrates for failure to predict penicillin, or Galileo for not knowing all the planets? What is more pertinent is that Freud recognized more than we credit him. Thus, already in "Little Hans" in 1909, he would state that "The ego is always the standard by which one measures the external world, one learns to understand it by means of a constant comparison with oneself" (107). The ego was already an important component in his understanding the relation between self and other, and the importance of externality, that is, the importance of object relations. He indicated that the ideas of sex and object are so interwoven, that they often prohibit a realistic appraisal of their individual roles. Therefore, it would appear that the "bond between instincts and object in sexual life as being more intimate than it really is" (110). This has both reference to the displacement of the sexual instincts to objects other than primary objects and also gives to the object an independent valence in psychic development. He indicated that "His (Hans, my insertion) affection had moved from his mother on to other objects of love, but at a time when there was a scarcity of these it returned to her, only to break down in a neurosis" (ibid., 110).

In the early days of psychoanalysis, the parameters regarding whom one treated and whether treatment with friends, relatives, spouses, or relatives of patients was sensible had not been delineated. This was just the beginning of this new science, psychoanalysis, and the treatment of patients. Much was to be learned. Hans's father carried on the treatment in consultation with Freud and had been a member of the Wednesday evening scientific meetings. Frau Graf had been in treatment with Freud. That we can recognize the difficulty in discussing the family ethos is self-evident. However, is it not acceptable that Freud focuses only on a particular aspect for teaching purposes and elucidation of certain theoretical points that would not be a threat to the family's cohesion and privacy?

We cannot totally exculpate Freud, for as we read his case studies it is evident that the mother played a much less significant role than the father in his theory. Perhaps this was due to the culture of his times—a patriarchal culture, but we could also hypothesize that possibly Freud repressed his own deep attachment to his mother despite his uncovering the importance and primary role of the Oedipus complex in the neurosis and despite his self analysis. Yet, in this treatment, Freud certainly recognized the deep attachment of Hans to his mother. The focal point of Freud's presenting this case was to explicate the development of Little Hans's phobia, its component parts, the underlying etiology, that is, the Oedipus complex, and the role of sexuality and aggression in the child's relation to both parents and the role of conflicting identifications.

Little Hans had developed, first, a fear of a horse biting him, then elaborated into a fear of a horse falling down and parallel with these, his fear of going outside even when accompanied by his mother. Freud's interpretation regarding these phobias leads us directly to the Oedipus complex. The analysis carried out by the father in consultation with Freud takes us through the maturational phases of his genital desires in relation to his primary objects. We observe a very powerful attachment to his mother, the desires to "coax" with her, and his fear of losing her, "the object of his desire." Though Freud emphasizes the biological stages of development, for example, the anal, phallic and genital, his primary focus is upon the objects in this boy's life. Thus, we learn of Hans's deep love for his father, his ambivalence to this loving object due to his rivalry, and guilt because of his wishes to do away with the father and replace him as the mother's sole lover.

Speculation by his critics would place greater emphasis on pre-Oedipal conditions in Hans's life and the basis of his fears in relation to the mother. Is it not possible to conceive that the nature of the Oedipal conflicts, the state of a child's ego development and ambivalence to his objects may also be a powerful motive force to produce a phobia? Did not Freud pave the way for understanding very important elements that constituted the phobia in this very young child?

CASE OF DORA: FRAGMENT OF AN ANALYSIS OF A CASE OF HYSTERIA

Much criticism has also been leveled at Freud for his manner of treatment of this young girl (Kanzer, 1980; Glenn, 1980). For most of the critics, the judgment that Dora in actuality was an adolescent girl whom Freud treated and behaved toward as an adult woman appeared reprehensible. One can only comment that so, too, was Juliet (Romeo and Juliet, Shakespeare) only fourteen. Did not Shakespeare treat her as a woman? Can we really know the psychic maturity of individuals in earlier cultures? Do we not do an injustice to predicate our evaluation of the past as an exact replica to our own times? Perhaps we ought to trust the author's understanding of his characters and their maturity as a valid expression of the period in which they lived. Therefore, to accuse Freud of "insensitivity" displays a touch of hubris on the part of his critics, and their failure to understand a culture where eighteen-year-old girls were considered of a marriageable age and had far more familial responsibilities than in the present culture.

The second main criticism was that Freud seemed more sympathetic to her father, the adulterer, than to the betrayed daughter (Kanzer and Glenn, 1980). Again, the daughter is not a wife and, thus, Freud showed us the nature of her unconscious fantasies that were enacted by a very Oedipal young woman. Freud, himself, related that Dora, at times, reacted as though she was a betrayed wife rather than a daughter witnessing an unhappy marriage as she observed her beloved father's love affair with a woman to whom she was also attached. Freud's just appraisal of the father was apparent by his statement following Dora's reproaches against her father: "I could not in general dispute Dora's characterization of her father and there was one particular respect in which it was very easy to see that her reproach was justified" (47). At another point, Freud indicated that the father was " . . . one of those men who knew how to evade a dilemma by falsifying their judgment . . . " (44).

Dora was brought to treatment by her father at the age of eighteen due to a series of hysterical symptoms: dyspnoe, tussis nervosa, aphonia, taedium vitae, depression, and a letter that was found indicating her threat of suicide. The treatment lasted approximately three months and we must assume that it consisted of daily sessions except Sundays. Before Freud tells us the facts of the case, the intricacies of the various relationships, and the underlying conflicts, he commented:

> Her father was the dominating figure of this circle, owing to his intelligence and his character as much as to the circumstances of his life. It was those circumstances which provided the framework for the history of the patient's childhood and illness. . . . His daughter was tenderly attached to him, and for that reason her critical powers, which developed early, took all the more offense at many of his actions and peculiarities (26).

Freud had already introduced us to the relationship factors that dominate this case history. In the process of the unfolding history and symptomatology, we learn the primary factors that compose Dora's hysterical neurosis. The family composition consisted of the father, the mother, Dora, and a brother who was eighteen months older. The father, who plays a central role in this drama, is having an affair with Frau K., a beautiful younger woman who is a friend of the family. Herr K., the husband, is pursuing Dora who is in love with him, yet consciously denies this and scorns his overt sexual advances though she accepted his indirect advances of daily flowers and many gifts of jewelry. The mother, who is described as a neurotic housewife and rather uninteresting, seems to subtly conspire with the husband to deny his extramarital affair. Thus, also, do the parents deny the intent of Herr K.'s courtship of Dora.

On all levels, we witness a case of familial "foile adieu." Freud indicated that Dora was angry at her father and on bad terms with her mother. The brother, of whom we know little, seems to have taken the mother's side in the couple's quarrels and yet, at one point, wonders why Dora is so upset over the father's affair. He indicated that the father "got so little understanding from his wife and was entitled to some happiness" (54).

Dora's symptoms seem to have a consistent history beginning around the age of eight when she has her first attack of chronic dyspnoea. At age twelve, she began to suffer from hemicranial headaches and from attacks of nervous coughing. The headaches lessened through the years while the "tussis nervosa" continued. When she came into treatment, she was again coughing and together with the cough was a loss of her voice (30).

At age sixteen, Freud first saw Dora for a consultation and had recommended treatment that was not followed through until two years later. When he first saw her she was described as being:

> In the first bloom of youth—a girl of intelligent and engaging looks . . . but now, Low spirits and an alteration in her character had now become the main feature of her illness. She was clearly satisfied neither with herself nor with her family; her attitude towards her father was unfriendly, and she was on very bad terms with her mother. . . . She attended lectures for women and carried on "more or less" serious studies (31).

Very early in the case description, Freud gave a sense of the family relationships and interactions, and Dora's relationship to the parents. That he did not interweave the familial conditions and impact upon Dora with a theoretical exposition is a factor that will be discussed later.

In summary, the father was having an affair with Frau K. to whom Dora was at one point very devoted. Freud referred to this as a homosexual attachment. Initially, Dora aided the father in this affair by caring or looking after her children while her father was visiting Frau K. Herr K., as I noted, had been pursuing Dora since the age of fourteen. Freud leads us to believe that Herr K. was in love with Dora though he appeared to also be having an affair with the governess of his children. The two families frequently vacationed together and Frau K. nursed Dora's father through a serious leuetic illness. Thus, he uses this as an excuse to portray the relationship as only platonic. No one believed this. We have no knowledge of what Dora's mother thought or was concerned over except for her interest in money, jewels, and house cleaning.

The precipitating event seemed to result from an incident between Dora and Herr K. on their walk around the lake. Herr K. made a proposal to Dora, but before he could conclude his proposition, Dora slapped him and ran away. Several days after this incident, she told her mother of the encounter. Herr K. denied it and accused Dora of fabrication and occupied with sexual fantasies that are later corroborated by his wife. The father believed the Ks and thus, by his collusion, could justify his own affair with Frau K. Dora again felt betrayed by her father and, further, experienced betrayal from Frau and Herr K.

That Dora rejected Herr K.'s advances, though she was in love with him, was primarily due to the jealous tale of the governess who was hoping for a commitment from Herr K. The provoking words in this scenario were "I get nothing from my wife." It was these words that caused Dora to slap Herr K., and view him with distrust. "He spoke to me as though I were the servant girl" and, thus, emerged the drama. Dora was also enraged with her father and insisted that he give up Frau K., which he refused.

The case history reads like a Shakespearean play with vengeance, betrayals, jealousy, love, and hate. In this scenario, we have objects, sex, triangles, quadrangles, hetero and homo-sexual loves, and the intertwining of love and desire. That Freud is focused on defining the structure of symptom formation, the use of language as switch words that hide meaning, the defense mechanisms of reversal, repression, displacement, and the role of dreams, was clearly evident. To follow his analysis of the development and representation of Dora's symptoms is to be engaged in a brilliant exegesis of a process. Freud presented us with an array of motivations for neurotic illnesses such as infantile sexuality and Oedipal rivalry. These infantile wishes, not adequately resolved by either repression or sublimation, can continue to ferment into an adult neurosis. Freud further addressed Dora's rivalry and jealousy of her mother and the ensuing guilt and self-reproaches that are operative in Dora's unconscious and motivate her behavior (49, 52, 55).

That the role of sexuality is a strong component in this case, and in Freud's formulation of the meaning of the symptom formation, does not detract from Freud's explication of the object relationships and import that he gives to them. Yet, may we accuse him of not recognizing or not considering sufficiently, as part of his theory and treatment, that aspect of the Oedipal conflicts where the mother may also be in rivalry with the child or a pre-oedipal mother who was uninterested in her child and gives the child to the governess or to the father? What role did Dora's mother play in the etiology of her symptoms, in her identification as a woman, and in her ambivalent object choice? How would Freud have understood the many factors concerning Dora's symptoms if he would have stressed the relationship between Dora and her mother aside from the Oedipal jealousy?

Further, we may question if the mother gave Dora to her father as a substitute for herself and also gave him Frau K. What would the analysis have looked like if these factors had been introduced? It is necessary to note that this analysis took place in 1899, very early in the history of psychoanalysis. Yet, Freud showed such brilliant insights into the role of sexual development and sexual love, that is object love in psychic development. Can we really give an exact measurement to an "object" interpretation or "drive" interpretation in both qualitative and quantitative terms? Both are necessary and the nature of the symptoms will determine, in large part, the interpretation at a particular point in the treatment.

To conclude, there was Dora's negative transference of which Freud became aware, a little too late to use but, for the future, a revelation. Was the material that she fed Freud simply a ruse to give him what he wanted and, in the end to defeat him by leaving? As a treatment patient, she foiled him but, as a source of a wonderful theory, Freud and the future were the benefactors.

CASE: "THE RAT MAN"— NOTES ON A CASE OF OBSESSIONAL NEUROSIS

In the very first session after the patient had revealed a number of intimate details regarding his sexual life, Freud inquired as to what made him "lay such stress upon telling me about his sexual life"—a rather interesting question from an analyst supposedly only interested in the sexual life of a patient. The patient replies that he knew his work. Yet, it turned out that he had only browsed through *The Psychopathology of Every Day Life*. Perhaps, Freud had become known as the "sex" doctor in Vienna, and thus, the patient was bringing what he thought most interested him or could it be that sex was what most interested the patient. The history of the patient's sex life unfolded through his associations, dreams, and current behavior. Yet, the most important aspects of the case that were revealed from the detailed insights into his compulsions were the degree which the Rat Man's conflicted relations came to the fore with both his father and the woman he loved, that was, his object relations. We observe Freud working from the "here and now" with the patient, moving to the past, the infantile, the pubescent, and again to the present. The major focus in the treatment was on the "Rat Man's" ambivalence towards his objects, his conflicts between love and hate. The quality of the drives and their energic force were implicit and explicit in Freud's exposition, but their relevance had meaning only in relation to his objects, his father, and his "lady."

Freud described the patient's sexual behavior in relation to his sister, Julia whom "he almost assaults," the dressmaker with whom he has sexual intercourse, and the various other women who attract him. The focus in the treatment is specifically oriented to the major issue regarding his ambivalently loved objects. Thus, we learn that to marry the woman he loves was to defy his father's wishes, a father who is no longer alive, but whose influence continues to be quite powerful. The mechanism of identification and love for him continue as a powerful influence on the "Rat Man."

As Freud unravels his patient's "Rat Obsession," we observe that the symbolism and constructs regarding rats follow many associative pathways: money, children, penis, his father's debts as a soldier, and the patient's lust for other women. Freud indicated:

> In his obsessional deliria he had coined himself a regular rat currency. When, for instance, in reply to a question, I told him my fee for an hour's treatment, he said to himself. . . . "So many florins, so many rats." Little by little he translated into this language the whole complex of money interests which centered round his father's legacy to him; that is to say, all his ideas connected with that subject were, by way of the verbal bridge 'Raten (installments)-Ratten (rats) carried over into his obsessional life and brought under the dominion of his unconscious (213–14).

Though the patient's obsessional neurosis became pronounced about four years prior to his beginning the analysis, the precipitant event was an obsession regarding rats and a demand to pay back some 3.8 florin to Lieutenant A., that the patient had to know was a false and incorrect demand. What emerged from this fabulous tale is a man worn out emotionally by a dilemma of whether or not to marry the woman he loved. To marry this woman would meet with the disapproval of his mother, but more pertinent for the patient was the opposition of his father, though already deceased by nine years. The lady, a cousin, was poor and an orphan living under the protection of relatives. The patient was offered another lady of wealth and excellent connections and, thus, the choice of his family. To marry his love meant relinquishing money, powerful connections and, most important, opposing his father whom he continued to confront as a "live ghost." His father, though poor had married a woman of wealth and connections, and thus, wished his son to follow this path. The patient was torn between loyalties. Yet his lady was not un-blemished in his mind; she was unable to have children due to the removal of her ovaries and twice had rejected his proposals. Therefore, his desire to have children would be precluded by this particular union. This wish and conflict were expressed in his rat obsession, rats signified children.

Freud did not negate the aggressive component in the rat man's conflicts. The early infantile sadism that had been repressed re-emerged in obsessive thoughts of rats boring into her anus that also satisfied his anal eroticism. In spite of the powerful repressed infantile sexual and sadistic wishes that were components in the development of the patient's obsessions, the analysis of these was secondary both causatively and interpretively for Freud. His main focus with the patient, as I have indicated, was on his object relations, his conflict with his objects, love for his father, and the love for his lady.

Any discussion of Freud as a neutral and removed analyst must take into consideration Freud's shaking hands with the patient, his engagement in much explanatory discussion, his urging him to show a picture of his lady, tell him her name and, finally, his feeding herring to the Rat Man. Much of Freud's behavior entered into the patient's transference dreams and enactments.

It is very difficult not to exult Freud for his integrated understanding of the biological role of drive and drive development in the human psyche, but also for his composite interweaving of drive and human relationships that permeate his case studies. Freud indicated,

> It follows from the nature of the facts which form the material of psychoanalysis that we are obliged to pay as much attention in our case studies to the purely human and social circumstances of our patients as to the somatic data and the symptoms of the disorder. Above all, our interest will be directed towards their family circumstances ("Obsessive Actions and Religious Practices," 1907, in *Collected Works*, Vol. II, 25-26).

"THE WOLF MAN"— FROM THE HISTORY OF AN INFANTILE NEUROSIS

In the comprehensive case study of *The Wolf Man* (1918a), we find an omission that can give some validation to the criticism regarding Freud's neglect of the "object." This is the period of Freud's technical maturity. He has presented a generalized picture of the "Wolf Man's" family, his beloved nursemaid "Nanya." and a somewhat more detailed picture of the patient's relationship with his sister. Yet, in regard to his father and mother, we are somewhat deprived of an indepth knowledge of their personalities and the nature of their more specific relationship to the patient. We may define the issue in pre-Oedipal or Oedipal terms, depending on our theoretical predilection. Pertinent issues of attachment that are recognized in relation to Nanya, the intricacies of his relations with his sister, identification, and object choice in regard to the father, are not discussed in relation to his mother. This omission leaves us with some questions regarding the role of his mother. It is especially important since Freud had indicated that the "infantile experiences are by themselves in a position to produce a neurosis" (54).

Dreams, psycho-sexual phases, obsessional thoughts, and involvement with his intestinal disorders were the source of much vital and vibrant interpretations; yet, as I have indicated, not much of the interaction with the parents, especially with his mother, was presented. Perhaps, the maturational phases, by this I mean, the psychological and sexual phase development, that are an inherent hierarchical process in human beings were the primary focus for Freud. He (1918a) indicated: "phylogenetically inherited schemata, which like the categories of philosophy, are concerned with the business of 'placing' impressions derived from actual experience. I am inclined to take the view that they are the precipitates from the history of human civilization. The Oedipus complex which comprises a child's relation to his parents is one of them . . . " (119).

Further, he indicated that the schema may triumph over the individual's experience, "as when in our present case the boy's father became the castrator and menace of his infantile sexuality in spite of what was in other respects an inverted Oedipus complex. A similar process is at work where a nurse comes to play the mother's part or where the two become fused together" (ibid., 119). I have emphasized, these statements as they point to the mutual interconnections between instincts (drives) and object relationships, concepts that permeate all of Freud's thinking.

At this point in the history of psychoanalysis, Freud was still very much concerned with establishing the role of psychoanalysis as a means of appropriate treatment for the neurosis and the value of its methodology. In addition, he was focused on the nature of the unconscious, infantile sexuality, its impact on future development, and the importance of repression and dreams. Object relationships, an established premise in his mind, took on a secondary role in this exegesis.

Freud was still carrying on a theoretical debate with Jung and Adler. Jung had disputed sexuality as a drive state and imputed to libido, a concept of energy devoid of sexuality. Adler who introduced the concept of aggression, mitigated its instinctual aspect and preferred to term it as a drive for mastery, therefore, focusing more on the psychological aspects rather than the biological force. Increasingly, he moved away from consideration of the sexual drive. Freud's primary interests at this time were concerned with the unfolding of the sexual drive, its importance in childhood development, contribution to the neurosis, and the specificity of symptom formation. The actual interaction with the parental objects, though generalized in his case presentation, were not the main focus of his work or primary interest. Nonetheless, this missing element should be noted, despite Anna Freud's apt comments, as noted earlier, particularly as Freud indicated he was discussing only those aspects of the case that dealt with the infantile neurosis (in *Collected Works*, Vol. III, 474).

Freud stated that his primary concern in presenting this case study was to explicate the relationship between a childhood neurosis and the adult neurosis. He had earlier stated that a "certain correspondence between the developmental phases of the ego and the libido; indeed a disturbance of that correspondence might provide a pathogenic factor" (Freud, 1916–1917, 352). Thus, certain situations in childhood, whether real events or phantasies, influence the adult neurosis and require bringing them to "consciousness," either though retrieval of memories or constructions. "I am of the opinion that *the influence of childhood makes itself felt already in the situation at the beginning of the formation of a neurosis, since it plays a decisive part in determining whether and at what point the individual shall fail to master the real problems of life" (1918a, 54).*

"THE WOLF-MAN" — FROM THE HISTORY OF AN INFANTILE NEUROSIS

The Wolf-Man entered treatment with Freud in 1910 at the age of twenty-three and terminated treatment in 1914. He had another short analysis with Freud of approximately four months in 1924 and a second analysis with Ruth Mac Brunswick from Oct. 1926-Feb. 1927.

His ego functioning was impaired and he traveled with a companion who cared for him. The adult onset of his disturbance occurred in his eighteenth year, precipitated by a gonorrheal infection. Prior to coming to Freud, there were many attempts at treatment, stays at sanatorias, psychiatric visits, even several sessions with Professor Kraepelin, the world, renown psychiatrist. All of these attempted treatments proved futile.

"The Wolf Man," of Russian birth, was born into the landed aristocracy. His family owned several large estates and had not the Russian Revolution intervened, he would have remained wealthy for life. He had an older sister, two and a half years his senior, who appeared quite precocious, and as a child was superior in her achievements and functioning. She was quite cruel to him as a child and sexually seduced him. He rebelled against her advances as they placed him in a passive position. He, thus, turned to his nurse-maid, "Nanya," asking her to "touch his penis" and gratify him. Unfortunately, the sister committed suicide by taking poison at age twenty-one. At the time, brother and sister had been reconciled and he was very distressed by her death, though he also experienced the feeling as "now I am the sole heir" to the family wealth.

His mother who suffered from abdominal problems since his infancy was barely involved with him and turned his care over to the nurse-maid, Nanya, whom he loved and who was devoted to him. The patient's father suffered from a manic-depressive illness that through the years became more pronounced and he was increasingly absent from the home. In the patient's early years, he was very close to his father and considered himself the favorite child but later felt displaced in the father's affections by his more talented sister. A good deal of the care of the Wolf Man was left to his nurse-maid, governesses and, later, to tutors. Though from his later history, one has the sense that he had a close relationship to his mother with whom he lived after the death of his wife. His father died when he was twenty-one.

Freud noted that around age two, "The Wolf Man" developed a loss of appetite and only wanted sweets. About the age of three and a half (or three and three quarters), he turned from a very sweet tempered child into a very "naughty" boy, tormenting all, including his beloved "Nanya" and small animals. Subsequently, he developed a wolf phobia that was then transferred to lions. At age four, this turned into obsessive piety, a series of rituals of going from room to room and kissing the holy pictures. His mother, who was deeply religious, helped in the development of his piety and religious neurosis. In adulthood, his obsessional neurosis fully emerged.

"The Wolf Man's" sister had played an important role in the development of his neurosis. Her aggressive behavior as tormentor, and sexual seducer contributed to his struggles over his passive, masochistic wishes and his active masculine desires. As a competitor for the father's affections she represented the successful rival for the man. His unconscious identification with the female aroused homosexual conflicts that further contributed to his passive wishes. Unconsciously, in order to denigrate and defeat his sister, he chose women who were of a lesser intellectual status, generally domestic servants. Though, once the relationship began, he placed himself in a passive, masochistic position.

The analysis as summarized by Freud evolved from an understanding of his early oral phase to the anal sadistic phase, to increased emphasis on the sadistic and masochistic factors, the final genital phase, and his regression to earlier phases of development. In each of these phases we observe the multifaceted identifications with his parental objects. Though, again, we feel somewhat deprived of a more detailed interaction of the Wolf Man with his parents and the nature of their relationship.

Perhaps the centripetal moment in the treatment was the remembrance of a childhood dream and the interpretation and construction of events that led to the major insights into the Wolf Man's neurosis. The dream acted as a watershed from which flowed the tributaries in various directions and velocity, and then coalesced into a comprehensive picture. As Freud indicated "dreaming is another kind of remembering" (51). The dream (Freud begins the chapter [ch. IV, "The Dream and the Primal Scene"]) was a crucial factor in uncovering the Wolf Man's central conflicts and, more significantly, emphasized the import of the primal scene in children's lives. He indicated that its importance played a role no matter whether it was merely a fantasy or a reality. The dream as reported by "The Wolf Man":

> I dreamt that it was night and that I was lying in my bed. (My bed stood with its foot towards the windows; in front of the window there was a row of old walnut trees. I know it was winter when I had the dream, and night-time.) suddenly the window opened of its own accord, and I was terrified to see that some white wolves were sitting on the big walnut tree in front of the window. There were six or seven of them. The wolves were quite white, and looked more like foxes or sheep-dogs, for they had big tails like foxes and they had their ears pricked like dogs when they pay attention to something. In great terror, evidently of being eaten up by the wolves, I screamed and woke up . . . (51).

The meaning of this dream occupied many sessions and became, as Freud indicated, a recurrent theme and subject of the analysis for several years. A brief synopsis of the dream will provide a good deal of understanding about "The Wolf Man" both as a child and as an adult and will help to elucidate his underlying struggles. The wolves were symbols for his father, the frightening wolf who will gobble him up, a regression to orality and also, the castrating wolf of the Oedipal phase. However, the wolves also represented his mother. From the tale of the tailor and the wolf, we learn that the tailor pulls off the wolf's tail and, thus, represented his castrated mother with whom he also identified and wished to replace her in the relationship with his father. The wolf dream also provided an interesting by-path into the role of the primal scene and its impact as observed by him at age eighteen months.[1] The primal scene, through the mental mechanism of "deferred action," resulted in excessive stimulae and contributed to his conflicting sexual wishes, ambivalent libidinal objects and identifications. Further, the many associations to the dream brought forth his phobic fear of wolves, memories of touring the sheep pasture with his father, a number of stories regarding wolves, and his conflicted relationship with his sister.

Fundamentally, "The Wolf Man's" ego deficits stem from his failure to integrate his sexual identity into a more cohesive whole. Freud indicated that: "Thus the result of the dream was not so much the triumph of a masculine current, as a reaction against a feminine and passive one" (112). This flew against what Freud called "his masculine narcissism." The struggles between active and passive sexual wishes that pervade his identifications, that is, masculine or feminine almost equal in force, and his ambivalence regarding his object (sexual love) choices pervade the entirety of his mental and emotional life. His love for his father and identification led to his masculine identification and, thus, the active mode of masculinity. This path was clouded by an equally strong identification with his mother and his taking on the role of the passive feminine position in relation to his father. This passive feminine role ran contradictory to his strong narcissistic perception of himself and investment in his penis. To be feminine is to be castrated; and it was this fear of castration that was the primary source of his anxiety and defenses. Freud indicated: "his fear of his father was the strongest motive for his falling ill, and his ambivalent attitude towards every father-surrogate was the dominating feature of his life as well as his behavior during treatment" (1918a, 32). Freud's summarization stated: "His childhood had been marked by a wavering between activity and passivity, his puberty by a struggle for masculinity, and the period after he had fallen ill by a fight for the object of his masculine desires" (118).

That Freud neglected a more detailed analysis of "The Wolf Man's" relationship with his parents is certainly a fault, and indicated that the object relationships were a secondary consideration in his formulation of the neurosis. Yet, it cannot be denied that objects and identification with them were significant aspects of his theories.

I cannot end this case discussion without some reference to the Wolf Man's own words, especially, since we are fortunate to have a recorded history of his treatment with Freud. He will show a very different Freud, an image quite contrary to the characterization of Freud as distant, doctrinaire and working within a one-person system (Aron, 1995). "The Wolf Man" stated:

> In my analysis with Freud I felt myself less as a patient than as a co-worker. . . . This feeling of "working together" was increased by Freud's recognition of my understanding of psychoanalysis, so that he even once said it would be good if all his pupils could grasp the nature of analysis as soundly as I (Gardiner, 1971, 140).

At other times Freud spoke to him of his love for antiquities. Statutes, pictures, and plaques adorned his wall and office. "Freud himself explained his love for archeology in that the psychoanalyst, like the archeologist must uncover layer after layer of the patient's psyche, before coming to the deepest most valuable treasures" (Gardiner, 1971, 139). Freud also shared personal stories and spoke of his children with the Wolf Man. The most human of anecdotes related by the Wolf Man about Freud occurred when he remembered the time that he constantly talked about his wish to be with his fiancé who lived in another country: " I was always raising this question anew, and I remember that once—evidently Professor Freud was in a specially good humor that day—he raised his hands above his head and cried out pathetically: "For twenty-four hours now I have not heard the sacred name Therese!" (Gardiner, 1971, 85).

Unquestionably, we may have many thoughts regarding Freud's treatment methods, a host of ideas about his interpretations, and mode of exploration, but one thing is undeniable, he was emotionally involved with his patients, and as the Wolf Man stated, "Freud was no stranger to the "human, all too human" (149). Neither the patient nor his object relations went unrecognized by Freud.

NOTE

1. Freud deals with his own skepticism regarding this age of eighteen months and questions the child's capacity for memories at this age. By close analysis of the Wolf Man's history, he concluded that this memory provided an impression and considered it as a process of a "deferred action."

Chapter Three

Klein's Object and Drive Theories

A Perpetuated Myth

A review of Klein's work and its impact on the British psychoanalytic community confronts one with an amalgam of political, economic, and personal factors that at times defies a rational understanding. Further, that current "object relations" groups continue to consider Klein as an object theorist is perplexing. Klein, as I will demonstrate from her writings and case studies, is a drive theorist. At times, her emphasis on drive constructs in psychic development often exceeds Freud's theories and interpretations.

Klein arrived in London in 1926 at the invitation of Jones to deliver a series of lectures and shortly, thereafter, relocated from Germany to Great Britain. That she soon became an icon of the British Psychoanalytic Society and her meteoric rise to fame in a society organized by Jones in 1913, that regarded Freud as its titular head is difficult to comprehend. True, Freud was still living in Vienna and did not come to Britain until 1938. Still, Jones's ties to Freud were very strong and, thus, it is somewhat of a quandary to understand his role in regard to Klein. Further, Jones was aware that there were theoretical differences between Klein and Anna Freud that had already emerged within the German psychoanalytic society when Klein was working and living in Germany. That these differences were probably due more to personality conflicts than serious divergences in the underlying theory is a strong consideration.

It is also conceivable that Jones's role in the Freud–Klein struggles reflected issues other than theory and attest to unknown motives that can only be surmised. That the theoretical differences between Freud and Klein, though significant, had become so controversial as to eventually cause a major rift in the British Society probably reflected issues over power and control (King and Steiner, 1991). One can only question why these differences, for example, the role of phantasies, the death drive, the early impact of aggression, the onset of the Oedipal phase, and the mode of interpretation did not create an atmosphere of scientific curiosity and excitement. Rather, the vitriol, aggression, and incivility marred the entire atmosphere of the society and, certainly, the character of many of the prominent psychoanalysts. Could we have expected better of Anna Freud, Edward Glover, the Schmitlebergs, Klein, Isaacs, and Joan Revere?

To the reader of Klein's oeuvre that she had been labeled the originator of object relation's theory is somewhat surprising and that Guntrip (1969) believed that "Object Relations Theory" was primarily the creation, de novo, of Melanie Klein is an evocative statement. He indicated that it was to her credit that an enormous advancement in psychoanalytic theory had occurred. Guntrip (1961, 1969) stated that Freud underestimated the importance of the object in psychic development. He believed, that Klein:

> Has truly sewn a new patch on an old garment in retaining Freud's instinct—theory and his particular terminology for endopsychic structure . . . thus Klein carries object—relationships right back through the Freudian so-called narcissistic and autoerotic phases to the beginning of the infant's separate body life. It is the importance, not of instinct but the earliest experiences in object–relationships, not of innate factors but of developmental experiences in the first two years, which her work emphasizes (1961, 216).

In regard to Klein's concepts on aggression, he stated that, "aggression itself elaborates and becomes a permanently active factor in the psyche. It can only be understood, therefore, not as an innate but as a developmental phenomenon, arising out of bad object relationships inside as well as outside the psyche" (216). Guntrip's understanding of Klein's theory appears contradictory to her stated ideas, regarding the role of aggression, an aspect of the death drive that she has always viewed as one of the basic innate drives. Her thought that what is outside is essentially a projection of the inside, that is, vicissitudes of the drive state at each developmental phase, again places Klein closer to Freud than the English Object Theorists. Further, her developmental phases adhered to Freud's stages: oral, anal, and genital.

I have focused on Guntrip as he was perhaps the quintessential analyst advocating object relations theory. I plan to show that in sharp contrast to Guntrip's conceptions, Klein's theories not only parallel Freud's hypotheses, but they are "essentialist," that is, instinct theories. That both Freud and Klein emphasized the maturation of the instincts, though in different time sequences, and that both believed that the instincts motivated human development is apparent in their writings. Though, Klein increasingly referred to the concept of objects, it was the internal object, the "good" and the "bad" object, which would become basic to her concept of ego structure and psychic functions. Her fundamental hypotheses claimed that drives and drive derivatives constructed objects that were first, internal objects.

Clearly, the object played a significant role for Klein as for Freud, yet what really was the nature of Klein's "Object"? Her object was not an internal representation of the object in the external world, that is, a reflection of the constituent elements of that object. Her object was not isomorphic with the external object. Klein's internal object represented a composite of internal drive derivatives that essentially affected the nature of externality, rather than the reverse. It is possible to conclude that Klein's object developmental phases reflect a "preformative" and phylogenetic theoretical postulate rather than an epigenetic one. In her 1957 paper "Envy and Gratitude," she indicated:

> I would not assume that the breast is to him merely a physical object. The whole of his instinctual desires and his unconscious phantasies imbue the breast with qualities going far beyond the actual nourishment it affords. . . . It is these phantasies and instinctual needs that so enrich the primal object that it remains the foundation of hope, trust, and belief in goodness (180).

Further, we may question if the object representation comprises an exact replica or an objective evaluation of the interaction between subject and object? Were subsequent internal object representations primarily the result of the impact of the external object relationship, and were the perceptions a replica of the reality object relationship? Many of her critics, most notably Glover (1933b, 1945), indicated that the external object relationships presented in her case studies were so modified by the aggressive and libidinal drive states that the internal objects reflected qualitatively, a composite of these drives rather than any interaction with the reality of external life. Her writings regarding phantasy explicate this point. They have become a trademark for a highly developed, ideational system (Glover, 1945) that appears to pre-exist prior to cognitive development or much interaction with the environment. The time factor and the nature of specific phantasies fully formed in the first months of life can further substantiate the conclusion that Klein does not fundamentally represent Object Relations Theory, as is currently conceived.

Glover (1945) contended that the Kleinian "system has broken through the limitation of metapsycholgy to postulate a bio-religious system which depends on faith rather than on science" (108) and that this system with its universal phantasy content, irrespective of the specific external experience or phase developmental stages, "is closer to a mythic–phylogenetic religiosity then to the neurogenesis of psychoanalytic theory" (106–107).

Makari (2008) indicated, that Klein moved from the complexities of " . . . inner and outer to just inner. She simplified her field of study and pursued the intrapsychic causes of childhood fear. . . . However, Melanie Klein did not bracket potential outer causes so much as to eliminate them. The developmental, traumatic, and environmental became increasingly irrelevant to her" (427-428). Though in latter years, she conceded that the outer world played some role, her focus on the purely internal had already been too entrenched to make a difference. Thus, ironically, it was Klein who had postulated the prime role of internal drive states in child development, almost in direct contrast to Anna Freud (1974[1922, 1927]) who had stressed the importance of the external environment, the parents and the school, as contributing if not more, at least equally, to the disturbance of children.

Mitchell's (1981) critique of Klein is most interesting from the perspective of both denying her drive derivative theory to explicating her contradictory position on both drives and object relations theory. Thus, he begins his paper with the statement that "Object relations theory has become one of the ubiquitous phrases within contemporary psychoanalytic literature. It is used variously to refer to: "theorists who have departed from classical tradition, like Klein and Fairbairn" (374). Mitchell then proceeded to state that Klein's reliance on the death drive certainly brings her closer to drive theory than object theory. He cited her statement "The child's fear of his early objects is proportional to the degree of his own aggressive impulses, and the specific nature of these objects in his phantasies is particular to his own instinctual makeup" (Mitchell, 374–398; Klein, 1933, 270). He further indicated that Klein's early internal world of infancy, that is, the paranoid position results from the child's aggression to the mother, a result of the death instinct turned outward. From these statements and quotes, it is difficult to reconcile his statement that Klein is outside of classical drive theory, though true her drive theories in infancy contradict Freud's developmental schema in regard to onset of phases. The nature and degree by which the instinctual drives infuse her view of object development cannot place her outside of the orbit of drive theory.

Laplance and Pontalis, both classical analysts, gave an interesting description of how classical psychoanalysis understands the "Object." In their book, *The Language of Psychoanalysis* (1973), they indicated:

> Psychoanalysis considers the notion of object from three perspectives: One—"in correlation with the instinct, the object is the means through which the instinct achieves its aim." Second—in "correlation with love and hate—the object is focused upon, and Three—in 'correlation with the perceiving and knowing subject" . . . is a recognizable entity by "all subject." (273).
>
> From a genetic perspective the object of psychosexual development as well as the subject passes through phases from pre-genital to genital, and at this phase the object is no longer "a mere correlate with the instincts." The object is now recognized by its "diversity and richness and instinct gratification is no longer its "sole raison d'etre" (276).

If we examine Klein's schema with that of Laplanche and Pontalis, we observe that Klein's object does not follow a maturational phase that correlates with drive, external object, and cognitive development, but is a genetic object suffused with drives, a phylogenetic entity much like Plato's "a priori" system. For example, Klein's four-month old infant has already achieved a nascent Oedipal phase as a result of instinctual processes totally unrelated to the infant's experience with the external object or even somatic development. This, despite her paper (1957) where she gave some recognition to the behavior of the mother, but primarily the internal object, is structured by the fusion of the "life giving" and the death drive. The external world of objects, the quality of the inter-relationship has very little impact on the developing infant. Her theory that this infant had knowledge of the father's penis inside the mother or an awareness of babies inside the mother can only be ascribed to a priori knowledge.

THE SEXUAL INSTINCT AND THE DEATH INSTINCT

Klein's writings can best be characterized by two phases: those from 1921 to 1926 and from 1926 to 1950 (Glover, 1945). The earlier papers adhered to Freud's schema of mental organization and his time sequence of psychosexual phases. This first period placed more emphasis on the role of the sexual instinct while the second phase emphasized the aggressive drive, that is, the death instinct. She takes for granted the role of the two drives in structuring psychic organization and though she shifts emphasis from the libidinal to the aggressive instincts in her later work, the drives are primary factors in all her conceptualizations. In this shift, she felt that the "destructive impulses were seen in better perspective a fuller light was thrown on the interaction of the life and death instincts, and, therefore, also the role of the libido in all mental and emotional processes" (1948, 41). In a paper (1952c) regarding the emotional life of an infant, she stated: "The emotional and mental processes during the first year of life (and recurring throughout the first five or six years) could be defined in terms of success or failure in the struggle between aggression and libido. . . . " (93). The clarity by which she explains the role of the two drives, even when referencing the object of either projection or introjection, makes it impossible to deny her status as a classical drive theorist. The child's inner world for Klein (1955b) consists of relations and "happenings" that are the product of the infant's own impulses and phantasies. Here, she gives some recognition to the good and bad experiences of the external world. Yet, it is the inner world of persecutory anxiety, a derivative response to the death instinct and the power of the libidinal drive that will determine psychic development and the quality of the relationship to the external object. Further, the "confluence of these drives" modifies the force of the death drive and its destructive power either to the self or the object.

In a discussion (1923b) of Freud's comments on Leonardo Da Vinci, she did not note the effects of his relationship to his mother or that he was an "illegitimate" child. Rather, she emphasized Leonardo's capacity to sublimate the strength of his instincts. She stated: "Thus, Leonardo's genital activity, which played so small a part as far as actual instinctual gratification was concerned, was wholly merged in his sublimations" (88). Sublimation, a concept for dealing with the sexual drive, was an important factor for Klein in resolving sexual conflicts and the effects of the quantitative force of the sexual drive. Symptom formation as she generalized in her discussion of Leonardo arose:

> Accordingly we should have to postulate a complementary series between the formation of symptoms on the one hand and successful sublimations on the other—these series include also possibilities of less successful sublimation. . . . In my opinion we find that a fixation which leads to a symptom was already on the way to sublimation but was cut off from it by repression. The earlier this happens the more will the fixation retain the actual character of the pleasures—situation and the more will it sexualize the tendency on which it has bestowed its libidinal cathexis. . . . (89).

In a very telling phrase regarding the significant role that the instincts play in her schema, she stated "when we consider at how big a sacrifice of instinctual energy the normal man purchases his health" (104), she is addressing the universal impact of the drives on mental development, health, and neurosis. Klein (1923b) in *Early Analysis* indicated: "In analogy to neurotic inhibitions, these which we may call 'normal' were evidently founded on a capacity for pleasure which was constitutionally great, and on their sexual-symbolic significance" (77). The results of psychoanalysis, in every individual case lead back to repressions of childish sexuality as the causes of subsequent illness. Instinctual stimulus does not arise from the external world but from within the organism itself. Not only did she regard the pleasure principle as a prime regulator in mental development but she considered the "main accent" in the pleasure principle to be placed on its "sexual symbolic significance," and therefore by "effecting a libidinal cathexis, augments in a degree which we cannot as yet determine the original disposition and primary pleasure" (77–78).

She is not addressing the object or object relations in regard to either neurotic inhibitions or normal development, but quite the contrary, her stress was on the role of sexuality, that is, the sexual drive that "draws repression upon itself." In her discussion of the relationship between repression and anxiety, we again observe how close she assigns the role of libidinal cathexis to "ego-tendencies and their subsequent repression, from which it can be discerned that quantitative factors also determine the emergence or suppression of anxiety" (80–81). Klein appears to follow Freud's first anxiety theory indicating that anxiety was the result of un-discharged libido, that is, libido that is converted into anxiety as a result of repression.[1] Further, in a footnote (81) she stated that even in cases of successful repression "in which the transformation undergone by anxiety makes it quite unrecognizable, it is possible to effect the withdrawal of very large quantities of libido." In her analysis of a number of cases she indicated that the "development of individual habits and peculiarities had been influenced by libidinal ideas" (81). These concepts certainly attest to the libidinal drive's role as a causative factor in suppression, repression, and anxiety.

THE DEATH INSTINCT

Freud's introduction of the "Death Instinct" (1920) as the second drive theory in contra distinction to his former position that of the "Ego vs. the Sexual Instinct" (1905), threw the analytic community into some dither and certainly created considerable controversy. Interestingly, Klein was one who had accepted this hypothesis without reservation, and further, made this concept a cornerstone of her own theories on aggression. In a sense, she had been Freud's best advocate of the "Death Instinct," though regrettably, she received little recognition from Freud. Like Freud, she viewed the failure to adequately direct aggression outward, that is, to externalize aggression to an object, as an internal danger, "of being destroyed by this instinct" (1933, 250). Sadism and masochism, vicissitudes of the death instinct, also became prominent concerns in her study of infant development. Her emphasis on these two derivatives of the drives was also consistent with Freud's theories.

Significantly, with the introduction of the death instinct, Klein's theoretical emphasis on anxiety began to change. She now attributed anxiety to the function of this instinct. Klein (1948) stated:

> Thus, in my view the danger arising from the inner working of the death instinct is the first cause of anxiety. From the beginning of post-natal life, destructive impulses against the object stir-up fears of retaliation. Persecutory feelings from inner sources are intensified by painful external experiences, and frustration. This discomfort arouses the feeling in the infant that he is being attacked by hostile forces. The infant endures monstrous and 'phantastic' images of his parents that are projections of his own aggressive instincts, and thus, give rise to anxiety (29).

Klein (1933) stated these projections resulted in the infant's fear of external objects, expressed symbolically by monsters. "The child's fear of its object and the imaginary attacks it will suffer from it adhere in every detail to the particular aggressive impulses and phantasies which it harbors against its environment" (251). The child's excessive fears not only "originate from the early fears of 'imaginary objects,' but also correspond to the amount of repressed impulses of aggression which exists between the child's fears and its aggressive tendencies" (249).

In examining Klein's theories on anxiety, it is possible to observe how closely she cleaves to Freud's death instinct. She very clearly placed anxiety under the aegis of the death instinct, a shift from her earlier acceptance of Freud's first anxiety theory, the failure of the sexual drive to achieve adequate discharge. This was in marked contrast to Freud (1926) who shifted to an object theory. Freud had modified his theory of anxiety and introduced the concept of "signal anxiety," the ego's response to the loss of the need gratifying object. Klein (1933) positioned the danger of annihilation, the internal working of the death instinct, as the primary source for the arousal of anxiety. The amount of aggression not directed outward posed danger to the self. Thus, excessive tension is set up within the ego that is felt by it as anxiety. Anxiety is not only created by internal fears of destruction, but then by its projection outward, the external fear of the object's hate. In contrast, Freud (1926) hypothesized that primary anxiety resulted from the danger of object loss. Initially, the infant experienced the loss of the need gratifying object; in later development, loss of the love object; and then the dangers from social or moral anxiety (the superego). For Klein it would appear that the danger resulted from fears of annihilation, that is, the function of the death instinct, while Freud focused upon object relations and the danger of object loss. Given the claims that Freud did not consider the object sufficiently in his metapsychology, this is certainly an ironic twist.

Though the libidinal drive provides the necessary impetus for the aggressive drive to be forced outward, it appeared that the death drive was more intractable and less pliable than the libidinal drive. Perhaps, it is the libidinal drive that is more easily invested in the object and is defined generally by more constructive than destructive forces. However, Klein's increased focus on the vicissitudes of the death instinct in all of her later writings is very evident. These destructive wishes, manifested at the very beginning of life, reflect the early onset of the death instinct as it affects mentation. Klein referred to this phase, as the paranoid position, a phase in which the death instinct is fully operative. Both the defense mechanisms of introjection and projection define the quality of the internalized object that effectively structured the ego and superego. The internal aim of the death drive is most dangerous for the infant. Thus, the projection of this drive from the self onto its objects and its re-internalization serves as both a protective and defensive measure.

What is most notable in her discussion of the death instinct is her neglect of any reference to the "Nirvana Principle"; a principle, that Freud (1920) considered an important aspect of the death instinct, the organism's need to reduce all tension to its lowest possible denominator and eventually to an inorganic state. This piece of theory had little theoretical interest for her. She accepted that aspect of the death instinct that had descriptive, clinical relevance and treatment implications.

The issue of ambivalence (Schwartz, 1989) as operative from the beginning of birth was an added area of concern for Klein. The fusion of the "two instincts results or gives rise to sadism. In order to escape from being destroyed by its own death-instinct, the organism employs its narcissism, or self regarding libido to force the former instinct outward and direct it to objects" (250). It is the fusion of the libidinal and aggressive drives that is responsible for the deflection of the death instinct outwards and for the ultimate establishment of a healthy ego structure. To Klein's credit, she has perhaps inadvertently expanded the discourse on the nature of the "Death Drive" rather than simple acceptance or rejection.

KLEIN'S STRUCTURAL THEORY—THE EGO, THE ID, AND THE OBJECT

Though Klein upholds Freud's tripartite structure of the mind, her premise regarding the nature of the ego and the superego varies in many ways from his. The superego will be discussed in a separate section as its development is so closely related to the death drive and, in many ways so complex that a separate discussion seemed preferable. Her definition of the Id as the watershed of the drives is akin to Freud's concept. Klein "regarded the Id as identical with the two instincts," that of the sexual and death instincts (1958, 243). Though, she mainly referred to the Id as a source, she at times referred to the Id as a more organized structure, such as describing the "sadism of the Id." Klein also would confess that at times she gave a rather loose definition in describing the Id as representing only the death instinct or as the "unconscious" (244).

Klein's description of the ego is an amalgam of organization, function, and defense. In the early papers, she characterized the ego as structured by the introjection of objects that were initially drive objects projected outward and subsequently re-introjected. The objects were split into the bad object and the good object and she regarded splitting primarily as a defensive measure to both protect the ego from anxiety and the 'good object' from destruction by the "bad object." Initially the object was a part object, the good breast and the bad breast, and as the ego metabolizes and integrates the objects, they become whole objects.

That Klein also referred to the process of internalization as a result of incorporation and identification (these processes occur almost simultaneously), it would appear that her objects were initially objects based in the external world. Yet, as already indicated, her objects were essentially phylogenetic objects. Eros and Thanatos, that is the life giving and the death instinct structure, the object that is first and foremost an internal object, that only later reflects the ministrations of the mother. Recall that for Klein, the development of the object occurred in utero, thus giving the ego an extremely early developed character. Since the internalized and externalized objects have already developed feelings of love and hate and basically are dominated by the aggressive forces with desires to destroy, the existent ego is quite advanced with established ideations and phantasies. Phantasy for Klein underlies the mechanisms of introjection and projection.

Klein's (1935) ego further functions as a defense. She stated, the infant: " . . . develops a greedy love and desire to devour this object and the mechanism of introjection is reinforced. Besides, he finds himself constantly impelled to repeat the incorporation of the good object—that is, the repetition of the act is designed to test the reality of his fears and disprove them . . . " (264). The ego is, thus, defending itself against his (infant's) cannibalism and against the persecutory objects.

> We know that, at this stage the ego makes a greater use of introjection of the good object as a mechanism of defense. This is associated with another important mechanism: that of making reparation to the object. . . . The ego feels impelled . . . by its identification with the good object to make restitution for all the sadistic attacks that it has launched on that object (265).

The question may be raised as to whether Klein's ego is formed by identification with different objects and their mode of functioning, or whether her ego is a composite of many different conflicting objects so that the ego acts as an auxiliary of the various objects, rather than an over-all integrative mental organization that contains object representations and identification? Klein also viewed the ego as constantly endangered by objects, that is, persecutory objects, "ready to devour it and do violence to it. In all sorts of ways they endanger both the ego and the good object" (265).

In a later paper (1957), she indicated that primordial anxiety due to the death drive provided an explanation as to why "the ego is brought into activity from birth onwards." It would appear that the death drive, more than the sexual drive, is responsible for the formation of the ego; we will also see this same concept in the discussion of the superego. Though Klein will allot to the "life instinct" as the ultimate source of ego activities, particularly those of uniting and binding of drives and objects, it is primarily the aggressive drive that is responsible for psychic structure.

Klein's objects as indicated previously are, first, part objects, the "first of these 'internalized objects,' . . . is a part object, the mother's breast. . . . The breast, to which are soon added other features of the mother, as an internalized object virtually influences ego development" (1952b, 58). She further stated: "A world of good and bad objects is thus built up within and here is the source of internal persecution as well as of internal riches and stability" (58). Though she gave recognition to external experiences with the object, it is primarily phantasies of the object that determine the real impact upon the ego. She indicated: "the perpetual interaction between the life and death instincts and the conflict arising from their antithesis (fusion and defusion) govern mental life . . . " (59). Thus, Klein's ego development and her conception of objects is essentially an intra-psychic process driven essentially by inherent drive interaction and only very secondarily by the interaction with the external world.

THE SUPEREGO

Klein's definition of the superego combines various theoretical constructs. The superego is a structure, a defense, and, at times, seems to act as a drive derivative. Klein (1933) maintained that the "super-ego would thus be accounted for by the fact that it is an offshoot of very intense destructive instincts, and contains along with a certain portion of libidinal impulses, very large quantities of aggressive ones" (250). She indicated that in the standard nomenclature, the full development of the super-ego is considered to have developed by five to six years of age while in her considered view the "super-ego is fully operative" from two and three quarters to four years of age. Though, she also claimed that the inception of the super-ego " . . . begins at the same time as the child makes its earliest oral introjection of its objects" (251). Since these first "imagos" are "endowed with all the attributes of sadism belonging to this stage of development and since they will once more be projected on to the objects of the outer world, the small child becomes dominated by the fear of suffering unimaginable cruel attacks from its real objects and from its super-ego (251). The younger the child the "more crushing the super-ego" and the child's feeble ego has difficulty in sustaining its "crushing effects." The child suffers from images and phantasies, "fear of being devoured, or cut up, or torn to pieces," that "evolve under the influence of the super-ego." Behind these images are parental figures.

She further concluded that the child's super-ego does not coincide with the reality picture presented by the parents, "but is created out of the imaginary parent or images of them which it has taken into itself." Secondly, the fear of the real objects, "its phobic anxiety-is based upon its fear both of its unrealistic super-ego and of objects which are real in themselves, but which it views in a phantastic light under the influence of its super-ego" (249). The superego in these formative stages exhibits "excessive violence," and the ego of the “small child is in danger of being overwhelmed by its ‘elemental force.’” It is quite apparent that Klein attributes the dominant factor in the development and in the function of the superego to the death instinct. This is not an object relations theory as the objects constructed by the infant’s phantasies do not result from the dyadic relationship with the mother, but are phantasies in Klein’s lexicon derived from the death instinct. These are preordained thoughts irrespective of external reality. It is difficult to conceive that any external or internal object relationship could induce the conceptual level of aggressive ideation, fears, and phantasies that Klein ascribes to an infant or very young child.

Klein, in ascribing the development of the superego primarily to the actions of the death instinct, differs from Freud’s construction of the superego. Freud (1923, 1927, 1928, 1929a, 1933) conceived of the superego as a mental structure developed primarily from abandoned object cathexes and idealizations. By means of the mechanism of identification with the parents and the parental authority, internalization results in the establishment of the superego. Though Klein did also say that the super-ego develops early in infancy by means of identification or “oral introjection” of the parents, she repeatedly indicated in her major writings that the superego was erected by the ego to deal with aggression. Therefore, according to this view, fear of death enters from the beginning into fear of the super-ego. Anxiety is aroused by the infant’s wish to devour the good breast (the mother) and the father’s penis and, by projection of these wishes, therefore, the infant fears retaliation, that these objects will devour him.

It would appear that despite Klein’s claim the full operations of the superego do not occur until about two and three quarters to four years, and that we have a rather sophisticated functioning superego in infancy.

THE SUPEREGO AND THE OEDIPUS COMPLEX

Klein indicated that in each developmental phase, the impact of the superego with its severity and aggressive force is evidenced. That the superego begins during the early oral phase, though in an incipient stage, makes it possible for her to consider the rise of the Oedipus complex at this same period. Thus, she will conclude that they “coincide.” Klein considered that the Oedipal phase began at about four months. The Oedipal conflicts paralleling each stage of development will provide a valence to the oral, anal, and genital phases (1933). The interweaving of each psychosexual phase with the developing superego and the Oedipal conflicts dominate psychic organization, behavioral, and phantasy expression. The anal phase portraying all the characteristics of anality, that is, its expulsive and retentive aspects, also influences the quality of the Oedipal complex and the Oedipal object. The aggressive behavior towards the external object in the form of sadism reflects characteristics of the anal phase. Masochism also reflects attributes of anality. Entrance into the genital phase puts the final touches on the Oedipus complex where the severity of the superego will influence the resolution of Oedipal conflicts. There is some inconsistency in Klein's dating of the onset and full development of the superego and the Oedipus complex. Nevertheless, she bases their origins extremely early.

Earlier, we made mention of the paranoid or what Klein also referred to as the schizoid-paranoid position; this is followed by the depressive position. It is in this state that guilt for the destructive wishes toward the object arose and the need for reparation. Guilt and remorse for destructive wishes to kill or to rob the mother of her babies and the father's penis inside her, all come to the fore about the fourth month of infancy. This period referred to as the reparative phase, a stage of an operative superego and the Oedipus complex. The wish to destroy the Oedipal object that is also a loved object is a factor in the solidification of the superego as a means of controlling the aggression directed to the object of both desire and hate. The response to the object is not determined by the essential nature of the external object nor the quality of its ministration, but primarily by quantitative aspect of the drive that gives valence to the object.

The question may be raised, can the object become such a highly developed entity, a result of internal assimilation by the infant, that such precise, projected emotions at approximately four or even six months are possible? Or again, is the object for Klein essentially a phylogenetic object, almost fully conceived in infancy and practically defined at four months by the libidinal and aggressive drives.

PRIMARY NARCISSISM

Klein's position on primary narcissism would seem to place her in the arena of object relations and not all within drive theory. Yet, I will show that her theories on narcissism are essentially phylogenetic. Klein (1952, 1957) asserted that primary narcissism, an objectless stage is non–existent since objects exist from the inception of birth. Recall at times, she stated that objects are already present in utero. Thus, Freud's theory regarding primary narcissism has little bearing for Klein. However, if we examine Freud's ideas on early identification that even precede object relationships, the idea of primary narcissism has some very important meanings. The object is taken in so that structure is beginning to develop for the incipient ego, as it establishes contact with the external world. The nature of the libido, that is, its quality, as it connects with the object, is narcissistic, based primarily on a need-gratifying basis and invested primarily within the ego to satisfy the self-preservative functions of the instinct. The object is not yet independent or differentiated from the self, yet the narcissistic libido is already in the process of becoming attached to the object. As I have shown in my discussion of Freud, there is no objectless phase. Rather, it is the quality and the function of libido and ego in relation to the object that is of importance. The nature of object stages, that is, narcissistic, auto-erotic, need gratifying, and object relatedness, all give a certain quality to the hierarchical stages of drives and object relationships. That Klein discards primary narcissism is not a rejection of drive theory; rather, her drives have already helped to constitute the object in utero.

CONCLUSION

Klein's theories on the object, though tantalizing for the object theorists as she repeatedly refers to objects, especially the internal object, bear little or no relationship to their theories. Her objects are phylogenetic, preformed in the infant's mind almost at birth with very proscribed libidinal and aggressive behaviors, phantasies, and stereotypical instinctual responses. Therefore, it is very difficult to deny the fact that Klein considered instincts as fundamental to structuring the ego, the self, the superego, and object representation. Schafer (1997) indicated in his book on Contemporary Kleinians, "I also hope to counter what I see is the growing tendency in the United States at least to include the work of the Kleinian group under the broad rubric object relations analysis. Contemporary Kleinians refuse to identify themselves with the "loosely assembled aggregate of approaches" (X11). To this we may ponder as to how to explain the early English Object Relations' evaluation of Klein as an object theorist.

NOTE

1. This paper preceded Freud's 1927 paper on "Inhibitions, Symptoms and Anxiety" where he modified his theory on anxiety. Anxiety was now essentially seen as a response to various phases of object loss. Nevertheless, Freud never fully abandoned his energic concepts in regard to anxiety.

Chapter Four

Klein's Case Studies

Klein's case studies of children both in her early and later writings provide sufficient evidence that drive theory and phylogenesis were fundamental concepts in her thinking. It is not the object or the interaction with the object that determined psychic development but the drives, the sexual and aggressive drives that influence object relations and affective discharge. Grosskurth (1987), Klein's biographer, who was quite sympathetic to her, indicated that in her analysis of her son Erick whom she presented as a case study (Fritz), she seemed to show little awareness of the "external factors" in his life. Nor did she take into consideration any of the very difficult situations that the boy was subjected to, and "in writing up the case history ascribed his anxiety as a result of repressed libidinal wishes" (97). This despite the fact that the boy had moved residences almost yearly, had been separated from his father due to the war, and ultimately suffered the parental divorce. After which, he had been sent away to a boarding school. We may hypothesize that Klein recognized the impact of externality, but that she was primarily concerned with the effects of the drives upon the external object. Interestingly, this same criticism has been leveled at Freud. Yet, it is not conceivable that Freud or Anna Freud with whom Klein was in conflict could have negated the degree that the external world impinged upon one's life, particularly the inner world of a child.

In her paper "On the Development of a Child" (1921), Klein raised the question "In how far are these complexes phylogenetic and innate, or in how far ontogenetically acquired?" Her answer appeared somewhat equivocal in that she gave some recognition to the family situation but rarely in the treatment was the family or social environment considered. For example, in discussing Fritz (i.e., Eric) she stated that "In the case of this boy, where threats were never used and where pleasure in masturbation was pretty frankly and fearlessly shown, there was nevertheless a very strongly marked castration complex that had certainly developed on the basis of the Oedipus complex" (48). Further, she indicated that "the foundations for his inhibitions and neurotic traits seem to me to reach back before the time even when he began to speak" (48).

There is no mention of the external environment in this treatment, and according to Grosskurth (1987), Erich was an unwanted child, and Klein was very depressed after his birth. Furthermore, the relations between Klein and her husband were strained. Perhaps one can forgive Klein for omitting the parental environment, since she was the parent, but to continue to neglect the effect that the social world had on Fritz is puzzling.

In her discussion of the symptomatic meaning of his "mild phobia," his fear of going outside and walking to school, Klein interpreted this as "symbolically expressing a desire for coitus, which is then followed by castration anxiety" (Grosskurth, 1987). Erich, according to Grosskurth, was accosted and bullied by boys on his way to school and subjected to their anti-Semitic slurs. We may validly conclude that his fears were quite justified by the reality situation that reinforced the anxieties underlying the Oedipal conflicts. Further, Klein indicated that his dislike of school "extended to his walk to school . . . this distaste revealed itself in the analysis as anxiety." When "in the course of the analysis pleasure had taken the place of anxiety, he related the following phantasy. The school children climb through the window into the classroom to the mistress. But there is one little boy who was so fat that he could not get in at the window, and had to learn and write his lessons in the street in front of the school. Fritz called this boy "dumpling" . . . the funny jumping "dumpling" (also called "Kasperle") proved to be a representation of the penis penetrating the mother's body. The school mistress, however, is also for him the castrating mother with the penis. . . . " I have condensed this material, but I believe it is evident that Klein's analytic approach and interpretive mode follows a path of pure instinct theory, and what critics have alluded to as classic psychoanalytic theory. What is perhaps so glaring in her treatment of Erich, was her failure to give recognition to the impact of what appeared to be a rather cruel external reality, the specific relationship with the parents, and his fantasies about them.

In reviewing the case of Felix who likewise is Klein's son Hans, we evidence a similar neglect of the role of real object relationships and the environmental impact upon the child. Felix, she stated, had a general dislike and disinterest in school despite his good intellectual endowment. He related a dream that he had at age of eleven. "He was on the road to school, and met his piano mistress. The school house was on fire and the branches of the trees on the roadside were burnt off, but the trunks were left standing. He walked through the burning building with his music mistress and they came out unhurt, etc." Klein interpreted this as an Oedipal dream. She stated, "Felix reveals a passive homosexual attitude toward his father, also a desire to penetrate his mother, and a sadistic conception of coitus. In relation to his classmates, he exhibits a good deal of rivalry and competitiveness." At the time of this dream, his headmistress had died! Klein made no mention of this in her interpretation nor did she acknowledge that the boy could possibly have been very anxious over this loss, and secondly, the school mistress may have represented a displacement from his mother, that is, Klein. Klein's frequent depressions were dealt with by long absences from the home while she traveled abroad for many months at a time. Her mother became the interim caretaker. Can we entertain the idea that not only did Felix feel abandoned, but that he experienced rage at her for leaving him? (Grosskurth, 1987) I am suggesting that the dream may also have had reference to aggressive feelings toward Klein alongside of the incestuous wishes that Klein interpreted.

Klein, again uses Felix as an example to explicate her point regarding Oedipal conflicts in her presentation of a *Case of Tics* (1925). For example, Klein indicated that Felix, by "turning away first from his mother and then from his father as loved objects was the outcome of his narcissistic regression and formed the basis of his asocial behavior" (110). Later, she stated that "A kind of identification with the father again took place, but was no longer successful because his characteristics were fused with the patient's own ego, and the patient's ego, loved by the father, emerges as the new loved object" (125).

Essentially, this paper is an exegeses on the role of masturbation, the defenses against it, coitus fantasies and incestuous wishes both passive and active in regard to his parents. What is perplexing is Klein's failure to connect the tic and other difficulties experienced by Felix to a rather cruel and denigrating father, or again to Klein's absences from the family. She stated in this paper that, when the father returned from the army, Felix faced a father who threatened him for what the father considered Felix's "physical cowardice" around his anxiety in gym and games. The father threatened punishments and thus, Felix, who had formerly been a very good student, becomes overly invested in sports, such as football, swimming, and gymnastics, and lost interest in his school-work. Further, the father's "insistence on supervising his homework" led to an aversion to learning that "made school a torture." Let us look at Klein's understanding of this boy's conflicts and defenses; she stated that, "At this period the struggle against masturbation was revived with great energy. The analysis of his passion for games with his dislike of school–work, was very much in the foreground during the first part of treatment, and showed clearly that games and other physical activities were to him a substitute for masturbation." I do not wish to preclude that the masturbatory conflicts and Oedipal issues were not significant factors in Felix's symptomatology, but Klein's failure to interweave the father's cruel and denigrating behavior must have had a great deal of impact on how these fundamental issues, that is, sexual and aggressive drives unfold in his psychic development.

The case of Richard (1945), whom Klein analyzed in the early 1940s, during World War II in England is an example of the manner in which she increasingly recognized the impact of the environment in her theoretical discourse. Yet, in her exposition of this case, her references to the real life situations that could give credence that she really considered the interplay between drive and objective reality is quite minimal. Thus, when she stated:

> there were difficulties in the family situation—as well as difficulties in Richard's early history—in my view the severity of his illness could not be explained by those circumstances alone. As in every case, we have to take into consideration the internal processes resulting from, and interacting with, constitutional as well as environmental factors; but I am unable to deal here in detail with the interaction of all of these factors. I shall restrict myself to showing the influence of certain early anxieties on genital development (372).

Could it not have been more advantageous for the reader to get an understanding of at least some of the environmental factors as they exert a dynamic influence upon psychological development? Since Klein had given some information on the family, a depressed mother who preferred his older brother, a somewhat loving but ineffectual father, a difficult marriage, and the trauma of the war years; an account of these factors as they impinged upon the Oedipal development and the identificatory process could widen our comprehension of the mutual interaction of the inside with the outside. Klein's final summation of this case gives no indication that the character of either parent or their interaction gave rise to the degree of aggression that he experienced with them and his brother. Did identification appear *ipso facto* without some interaction with the objects or did more specific acts and attitudes on the part of the parents influence this process? Except for one event, that of, Mrs. Klein interruption of the treatment by a trip to London was there any reference to Richard's reacting to a concrete situation. As a matter of fact, Klein dealt with this as a transference response rather than the boy's fear for her safety when she visited London during the period of the bombings. It is also possible that the degree of aggression that emerged in his drawings may also have been directed to Klein as a present object. Her current interpretations could have made him very angry together with her interruptions during the treatment.

I am suggesting that what was lacking in her treatment methodology was her failure to consider the specific nature of the objects interaction with the subject as well as projections and distortions in the subject due to frustrations and wishes in drive development. I do not argue with the validity of most of her interpretations from an abstract theoretical position, but rather her failure to be concerned with the environment in which her patients lived. Thus, when Klein interprets that his (Richard's) "hatred of children, as well as his fear of them, was partially derived from the attitude towards his father's penis" (393), there is absolutely no discussion regarding the attitude of the other children in his milieu to Richard and how they treated him. Richard, after all, was a displaced child during World War II, living in a different setting and possibly with a different class of children. To the degree that the "other children" evoke transference feelings related to Richard's father necessitates a bridging of the two separate objects, the father and the children.

To negate the role of the external world does an injustice to the methodology of psychoanalysis just as a negation of the internal psychological world influenced by drive development limits the depth of our analytic understanding.

Chapter Five

The Triumvirate

Ferenczi, Abraham, and Jones

In discussing Ferenczi, Abraham, and Jones, three giants of the early psychoanalytic movement, particular emphasis will be placed on their contributions and impact on psychoanalysis. Their relationship to Freud and role in the organizing of the psychoanalytic movement was fundamental to its success. It is not possible to discuss theory, politics, or the history of psychoanalysis without reference to them. Each had a crucial part in the development of psychoanalytic theory and in their respective influence on Freud and Klein.

The import of Ferenczi and Abraham on Klein as her analysts can be seen in some of her theoretical constructs. Klein's relationship to Jones, as colleague and analyst of his children and wife, resulted in a strong emotional valence between them. Jones's subtle conflicts with Freud probably played a role that underlay many of the struggles within the British Society. These struggles possibly clouded a more accurate understanding of Klein's basic drive theories that were incorrectly viewed as "object" theories. Further, that Klein rather than Ferenczi received the title of originator of "Object Theory" sheds some insights into the nature of the British Society and perhaps points a finger at Jones who was at odds with Ferenczi.

To understand relationships that are fraught with conflict, love, and hostility becomes obligatory in order to place in perspective a movement and the heroic figures that themselves suffer from the frailties of being human. Ferenczi, Jones, and Abraham often struggled with Freud over theories and methodology. Yet, it is possible to conceive that these struggles were abetted by jealousy and rivalry for his recognition as the favorite son, and perhaps, also, for political power, even who would succeed him.

Abraham, due to his premature death, was spared the painful episode of Ferenczi's rift with Freud and the deterioration of relationship between the Kleinians and the Freudians. Freud had analyzed Ferenczi; Jones had been in analysis with Ferenczi. The meshing of the personal with the theoretical could not be avoided nor could they escape the personal dilemmas regarding allegiance to either Freud or Klein, or in their struggles with each other.

Jones is of particular interest due to the complicated nature of his relationship, with Freud, Anna Freud, and Klein. Since Jones was primarily responsible for bringing Klein to England, one may well wonder at his motivation, as he was aware of the conflict between Klein and the Viennese, and also with some analysts in the German Society. Differences concerning the theoretical approach to the treatment of children had been brewing between Anna Freud and Klein, thus Jones's behavior is somewhat bewildering and becomes increasingly ambiguous in regard to the two rival camps. It could almost be inferred that he had two mistresses: Freud and Klein.

Freud wrote to Jones in 1927 (Jones, 1957, Vol.II) complaining about his actions:

> I do not estimate our theoretical differences of opinion as slight, but so long as there is no bad feeling behind them we can have no troublesome results. I can say definitely that we in Vienna have not infused any ill will into the contradiction, and your amiableness has prepared the way in which Melanie Klein and her daughter erred in this respect to Anna. It is true that I am of the opinion that your Society has followed Frau Klein on the wrong path, but the sphere from which she has drawn her observations is foreign to me so that I have no right to any fixed conviction (197).

Freud's tone was direct but not hostile, and presented an open mind to the disagreement both in theory, and the personal behavior that seemed insulting to Anna Freud.

Klein's (1941) attitude toward Jones is also indicative of his seemingly double role. She chastised Jones for bringing the Freuds to London: "I resented Anna settling here with a large and representative part of the Viennese group and thought that you had too little considered the disturbance to our work and also that you confronted us with a *fait accompli* . . . and I am also glad that Freud had a happy year in England in spite of the difficulties which Anna's presence give rise to here" (Freud-Klein Controversies, 228). It would be nice to think of Jones as the arbiter between the two warring groups, but history leads us to think otherwise.

Jones stands out among the three as the most influential figure in the history of the Psychoanalytic Movement. Abraham's death cut short an illustrious career both as a writer, theoretician, and the most eminent figure in the German Psychoanalytic Society. Ferenczi's writings and work had significant influence on Freud, especially his friendship in the early years. While the major theoretical writings at this period were largely influenced by Freud's postulates, cross-pollination certainly occurred and each of the three contributed original and important additions. Perhaps it is appropriate to refer to Eissler's (1971) comments that scientific findings and explanations will be added to, subtracted, and criticized even by the most loyal of followers.

Abraham's paper "Notes on the Psycho-Analytical Investigation and Treatment of Manic-depressive Insanity and Allied Conditions" (1911) was influential on Freud's later paper on "Mourning and Melancholia" (1917[1915]), that, in turn, influenced Abraham's paper "A Short Study of the Development of the Libido Viewed in the Light of Mental Disorders" (1924a). His paper stands out as a major contribution on the development of the libido and its impact on psychic disorders.

Ferenczi, who died in 1933, could best be described as the prodigal son. Ferenczi's work is currently witnessing a revival and has become the new hallmark of object relation's theory. His later work was intimately concerned with the therapeutic process that focused on the mother–child relationship and the nature of the object relationship in the transference and countertransference. He developed theories of mutual analysis between patient and analyst, a technique that he hoped would enable the patient to overcome the deep traumas of early childhood. His focus became even more concentrated on what he considered the seduction of the child by the adult. Given Ferenczi's writings on the mother-child relationship, one would have thought that the British Middle Group would have given him the title of "father" of object-relations theory. Why is this omission an interesting question? Edith Kurzweil (2012) stated: "Much has been written about Ferenczi's and Freud's relationship, their close personal friendship and theoretical disagreements, but not much attention has been paid to the influence of them on their surrounding milieu" (55). She further suggested that the absence on the European continent, in the UK, and the United States of his (Ferenczi) influence was due to cultural factors. particularly in the *Kaiserreich*, unfortunately, anti-Semitism played a part (ibid., 55).

THE THREE MEN

Jones

Jones was born in Gowerton (formerely, Fosfelin), a Welch province, in 1879 and died in 1958. Posterity will recognize him for his formidable three volume book on Freud and his role in the International Psychoanalytic movement. His biography on Freud is primarily a history of the psychoanalytic movement, its origins, the people who comprised the early movement, the struggles and conflicts, rivalries, heretics, and the tenacity of Freud and his followers to maintain psychoanalytic theory as both a science of human development and as a treatment method.

Jones had specialized in neurology and became acquainted with Freud's work in 1905 having read his case history of Dora in a German psychiatric journal. Through Jung, he was introduced to Freud in 1908 and soon was part of an inner circle of loyalist for whom psychoanalysis was recognized as a major scientific discovery. That this group had almost an apostolic-like character of which Abraham and Ferenczi were also a part in no way demeans the essence of its scientific endeavor. Freud's discoveries had a profound influence upon each of the people who surrounded him. They pursued this new discovery of mental life, the role of the unconscious, the impact of sexuality on psychic development, and the nature of psychic conflict, despite great odds and resistance in the culture and academic circles. At times, we, in the present, forget the heroic struggles that our psychoanalytic ancestors endured, the ostracism, the attacks, and financial sacrifices to follow this new understanding of human development and to establish psychoanalysis under the aegis of science (a difficulty that continues to plague psychoanalysis).

In 1913, Jones organized the London Psychoanalytic Society that remained in tact until 1919 when he disbanded it and re-organized the group apparently due to internal problems. The society was re-named the British Psychoanalytic Society (Jones, 1957, Vol. II) and he remained its president until 1944. He also served two terms as president of the International Psychoanalytic Society and founded the International Journal of Psychoanalysis. Jones's relationship to Freud was indeed an interesting amalgam of love, respect, deep friendship, and rivalry. His relationships with Anna Freud, Freud, Melanie Klein, and Ferenczi indicated an unconscious ambivalence and at times destructive behavior.

Despite his ambiguous relations with Freud, Jones must be credited for his untiring work on expanding Freud's theories and establishing structures for the teaching and the advancement of psychoanalysis. From 1908 through 1913, he lived in Canada and was responsible for translating and elucidating Freud's writings in the United States and Canada. He lectured widely, in Toronto, Detroit, Chicago, and New York. His lectures and papers delivered to various medical groups in the United States, Canada, and internationally, are exemplary for their clarity, and ability to explicate Freud's basic theories. Further, his style and structure bear a remarkable resemblance to Freud's explanatory methods.

The 1910 paper delivered before the Niagara District Association, St. Catherine, Ontario on the *Psychoanalytic Method of Treatment* explained the meaning and purpose of repression, the mode of operation of unconscious forces, and the development of neurotic symptoms. He stated: "Investigation by Freud's methods discloses the fact that every psychoneurotic symptom is a distorted expression of a repressed wish-complex. The wish itself on account of its unacceptable nature is buried in the unconscious, and the symptom arises as a compromise between it and various inhibitions of a more conscious order" (283).

He further indicated:

> Symptoms present in the psychoneuroses are the direct or indirect result of the non-absorption of various mental processes in the main stream of consciousness. Certain desires, wishes, thoughts occur to the patient, which not only cannot for various reasons be gratified, but which the patient refuses to acknowledge as a true part of his personality. Instead of healthy acknowledging their presence and then dealing with them, by either gratification or control according to the circumstances of the case, he fails to assimilate them, pretends to himself that they are not there, tries to forget them, to submerge or, as it is technically called to "repress" them (282).

The simplicity of style belies the depth of knowledge and his skill as a teacher. How easy for a group of novitiate physicians to follow his explanations by simple prose and logical process of cause and effect. This style, both didactic and empathetic, is indeed an unthreatening approach to the audience's own unconscious processes.

A paper delivered before the Detroit Society of Neurology and Psychiatry (1911) showed the technical skill by which Jones engaged his audience in the mental process of understanding the complex methodology by which diagnostic ability and treatment unfold in the analytic process. He begins by stating:

> Of all the problems relating to psycho-analysis the one that perhaps most forcibly arrests the student's attention is the question as to how it produces its remarkable therapeutic results. As is well known the treatment essentially consists in resuscitating the patient's past memories, and thus making him aware of his buried and unconscious processes: when they are laid bare the roots of the symptoms become manifest, and the nature, structure, and meaning of them are plain to both the physician and patient (300).

He further indicated:

> All this may be summarized in the sentence that, while an unconscious complex is necessarily in a state of dissociation, translation of it into consciousness signifies its assimilation. ———Under this term is included the conscious dealing with and absorption of the previously repressed thoughts, or rather wishes, together with the abreaction, analysis, and consequent diffusion of the accompanying affects (308).

Having indicated that the important goal or aim of treatment is to bring to consciousness the repressed forbidden wishes, Jones elegantly confronts one with the acute awareness that to make conscious what is unconscious "means very little in itself; to realize this knowledge through personal experience is quite a different matter" (308).

He then quoted a passage from Freud ("Uber 'Wilde' Psychoanalyse," *Zentralblatt fur Psychoanalyse*, Jahrg., "i." S. 1. 94) that stated "It is not the not-knowing in itself that is the pathogenesis factor, but the foundation of the not-knowing in internal resistances, which first brought about the not knowing and which still maintains it at present" (309). I have quoted these lines to emphasize the masterful quality of his teaching and to show how closely in style and form he adheres to Freud. The close connection that he makes with Freud makes it easy for his audience not only to absorb Freud's psychoanalytic thinking but also, to identify with him via Jones. One can understand the influence of Jones in spreading the theories of Freud and psychoanalysis by his engaging manner of discourse.

The relationship between Jones and Freud marked by mutual respect for their intellectual capacities unfortunately evidenced signs of strain due to their differences, mainly over political judgment and perhaps power. Freud was frequently harsh in his criticism of Jones and he certainly minced no words. Jones was generally correct in his evaluation of people such as Rank, Ferenczi, and Jung. Grosskurth (1987), quoting a correspondence between Freud and Jung, indicated that the relationship between Freud and Jones "was always to be one of wary fencing." Freud wrote that Jones was "very clever" but he (Freud—my insertion) was suspicious of the "motives behind the Welshman's interest in psychoanalysis" (155). In a letter to Max Eitingon (1927), Freud stated:

> I don't find Jones' behavior very puzzling. For a long time has been looking for "conflicts" or fights that hold the temptation to become independent from Europe and to establish his own Anglo-American realm something which he can not very well do before my demise, and he believes that he has found a good opportunity in the partial contradiction between Anna and Mrs. Klein. Perhaps we should add to it a partial anger with Anna dating since 1914, when she refused him (Young-Bruehl, 1988, f.n.,58,ch.4).

We must remember that despite the ambivalence that existed between Freud and Jones, their relationship lasted throughout Freud's lifetime, was enduring and deep, and withstood the battles over Jung, Rank, and Ferenczi. Indeed, between them lay buried many unconscious motivations and conflicts, and human foibles. Thus, we are at a loss to ferret them all out to find the ultimate truth. Perhaps the truth lies in all humanities' contradictions; thus, hopefully, we will be charitable in our judgments.

Ferenczi

Ferenczi was born in 1873 in Hungary and died in 1933 of pernicious anemia. He was particularly close to Freud perhaps due to his charming qualities and "speculative turn of mind." Unfortunately this close relationship from about 1908 until shortly prior to Ferenczi's death began to dissipate due to significant changes in Ferenczi's theories and unorthodox techniques. These theories, I believe developed to a point that Freud perceived as harmful to what was integral to the basic premises of psychoanalysis. Freud has received much criticism for his withdrawal from this friendship; criticized under the rubric of "demanding total allegiance to his so called gospel" (Ferenczi, 1926, 1933; Kurzweil, 2012). Interestingly, Balint (1968) claimed that Freud was saddened by this rift and that Ferenczi had failed to understand Freud's sympathetic attitude. Unfortunately, Ferenczi helped to perpetuate this myth. In his *Diary* (1933), he stated that Freud "could, for example, tolerate my being a son only until the moment when I contradicted him for the first time" (185). Yet, in 1926, in commemoration of Freud's seventieth birthday, Ferenczi criticized those who attacked Freud for demanding blind allegiance. He stated:

> I must testify that Freud often gives us perfect liberty for a long while, and allows great latitude to individual idiosyncrasies, before he decides to interpose as a moderating influence, or to make decisive use of the means of defense at his command; he resorts to the later course only when he is convinced that compliance would imperil the cause that to him is more important then anything else. Here he certainly admits of no compromise, and is ready to sacrifice, even though with heavy heart, personal ties and hopes that have become dear to him. In these things he is severe towards himself as towards another (16).

He also indicated "The fact that Freud has succeeded in schooling us to endure more of the truth would alone insure him the love with which a large and not unworthy section of humanity are thinking of him to-day" (17). These statements were another indication of the regard and admiration that Ferenczi had for Freud. A rather poignant letter that Freud wrote to Ferenczi plainly shows Freud's capacity to tolerate differences (Jones, Vol. II, Jan. 22, 1924).

He wrote:

> That as for your endeavor to remain in complete agreement, I treasure it as an expression of your friendship, but find this aim neither necessary or easily attainable. I know that I am not very accessible and find it hard to assimilate alien thoughts that do not quite lie in my path. It takes a long time before I can form a judgment about them. . . If you were to wait so long each time there would be an end to your productivity. That won't do at all. . . . Why shouldn't

> you therefore have the right to try if things won't work in another way from what I had thought (57).

Thus, for Ferenczi to attack Freud for authoritarianism and insisting on blind loyalty belies the reality of the facts. I think it was incumbent for psychoanalysts to fully evaluate the theories that Ferenczi was advocating and the changes in his personality more judiciously. As we examine Ferenczi's treatment of mutual analysis with the patient, it becomes evident that there were marked countertransferential aspects to this theory. Under the presumption of making the patient co-equal with the analyst an almost symbiotic quality develops between Ferenczi and the patient. Though, his stated attempt was to undo the early traumas experienced by the patient and thus, strengthen the patient's sense of self, this method appeared more as an "acting out" of his own personal needs. We can further speculate about Ferenczi's needs from his statement: "knowledge can be enlarged and deepened only by love" (*Diaries*, 17). To love the patient was an important element in his theory and, therefore, if Ferenczi was himself the patient, was this not also a means of acquiring love? I recognize that I am assuming a psychoanalytic role here, but as Hidas (*Ferenczi and His World*, 2012) stated in his review of Ferenczi "a piece of 'psychologizing' seems to be permissible."

Hidas had presented the hypothesis that the "trauma concept and the associated neocatharsis were a return of the repressed in his personal world" (111). I would further elaborate this analysis by indicating that Ferenczi, in attempting to reach the depths of his countertransference by using the patient as his analyst, was re-creating a transference situation to maintain the ties to the womb-like mother. His need to so engulf the emotional world, to re-create an umbilical cord between himself and the patient, speaks more to the denial of separation and distance from the infantile mother. He further wrote

> the continuous protests (from the deepest unconscious) that I do not in fact have many real empathy or the compassion for the patient, that I am emotionally dead, was in many respects analytically proven (in 'counteranalysis,' I) and could be traced back to deep infantile traumata . . . possibly to a traumatic event in earliest infancy (Hidas 113–114; *Diaries*, 85).

Hidas interpreted this as indicating that "It is obvious that the traumatic experiences of childhood have become conscious, or Ferenczi was convinced of their reality, only in the period of mutual analyses. . . . Trauma and catastrophe, as events that form both the individual and the species, are of utmost importance for Ferenczi" (114). Hidas indicated that Ferenczi's insights based on his experiences expressed the ideas:

> If the present process is to have a different outcome from the original trauma, then the victim of the traumatic shock must be offered something in reality, at

> least as much caring attention, or genuine intention to provide as a severely traumatized child must have. It appears, however, that even the child thus affected demands, as compensation for and counterweight to his sufferings, inordinate amounts of love, in both a qualitative and a quantitative sense (114, quoted from *Diaries*, 28-Ferenczi 1932a)

Ferenczi was increasingly preoccupied with the role of trauma in his patients' lives. The Diary (1985[1933]), written in the last year of his life, is dominated by the feelings for what he regarded as the basic affront to the patient and the underlying cause of neurosis and psychosis. Trauma is always an external event that causes psychic damage. In regard to trauma he stated:

> "Concussion," reaction to an "unbearable" external or internal stimulus in an autoplastic manner (modifying the self) instead of an alloplastic manner (modifying the stimulus). A neo-formation of the self is impossible without the previous destruction, either partial or total or dissolution of the former self. A new ego cannot be formed directly from the previous ego, but from fragments, more or less elementary products of its disintegration (Splitting, atomization). The relative strength of the "unbearable" excitation determines the degree and depth of the ego's disintegration (*Diary*, July 30, 1932, 181).

It is important to note that Ferenczi refers essentially to quantitative aspects of the destructive stimulus. Further, the destructive stimulus is generally a sexual seduction either an actual act or implicit psychological behavior. Ferenczi had a moment of insight when he recognized that one incident of rough treatment by his nurse in childhood as a result of soiling "gives rise to exaggerated tendency in me to attach too much importance to the wishes, likes, dislikes, of other people" (*Diary*, Feb. 16, 1932, 36).

I am aware that there is a danger in reading the Diary as a finished work, as a result of secondary processes, the conscious, integrated intellect, rather than thoughts closer to the unconscious and reactive to momentary impressions, emotions, and countertransferences. Thus, the Diary must not be regarded as the final product of Ferenczi's basic integrated thinking. With this caveat, I will permit myself another bit of analysis. First, the general feeling tone that the emotionality that runs through the Diary has aspects of what Freud (1930 [1929]) referred to as the "Oceanic" feeling, the ego merging with the object. The sense of wish to merge with the patient—to give exquisite love to reach such a perfect union and thus heal the patient to retrieve the patient who has:

> gone mad from pain, that is, those who have departed from the usual egocentric point of view, become able through their special situation to experience a part of that immaterial reality which remains inaccessible to us materialists? And here the direction of research must become involved with the so-called

occult. Cases of thought transference during the analysis of suffering people are extra-ordinarily frequent (*Diary*, Feb. 14, 1932, 33).

Or, his relating to a patient in mutual analysis:

> I warn the patient that I must tell her something extraordinarily painful . . . is she strong enough to listen to me? . . . With great resolve, the patient demands absolute frankness, whereupon I tell her that in fact I had deliberately exaggerated when I continually spoke of the success expected from her analysis. In reality I am often afraid that the whole treatment will go wrong and that she will end up insane or commit suicide. I do not conceal the fact that to have to tell her this was most painful and distressing for me, the more so as I myself knew only too well what it means to be faced with such possibilities. (reference to incidence in my early childhood.) Question: Was not the entire plan of "mutuality" conceived solely for the purpose of bringing to light something the patient had suspected in me and felt that I disavowed? Was it not an unconsciously sought antidote against the lies of her childhood? Full insight into the deepest recess of my mind, in defiance of all conventions, including those of kindness and consideration? (*Diary*, Feb. 20, 1932, 37).

Ferenczi must have assumed that therapists suffer similar traumas and that one must sink deep into the recesses of the unconscious to find that identical experience that resonates with the patient. Therefore, without this parallel experience, there can be no attunement. The demands that Ferenczi made upon himself and upon all therapists are Herculean and are not only impossible, but I consider anti-therapeutic for it negates the reality of separation of subject and object that patients must ultimately accept as part of the therapeutic process. Interestingly, this point regarding separation of the patient from the analyst is the very point that Ferenczi made regarding termination for the healthier patient.

The theme of death that occupies so many of Ferenczi's patients and his interpretations regarding their fading off to death, their self-destruction, and death like trances must have hovered over Ferenczi as immanent for him as he was so close to death due to pernicious anemia; indeed, he died in 1933 as he was writing the Diary. His description of patients' trance-like states, groaning, no pulse, breathlessness, cold bodies as death states, is another indication of Ferenczi's own preoccupation with his rapid decline and approaching death.

Ferenczi's later treatment techniques of mutual analysis, active therapy, and his almost obsessive need to give love to the patient, have never really been subjected to intensive scrutiny. That Freud rejected these methods and increasingly withdrew from Ferenczi has drawn more attention than a thorough objective evaluation of the situation. Jones referred to Ferenczi as psychotic in his later years and others have regarded his thinking as confused. Balint (1968) indicated that Ferenczi gave up the method of mutual analysis as it proved unsatisfactory and he began to consider the problems concerning the patients' inordinate demands for love.

Yet, despite this awareness, Ferenczi's major complaint was directed to the analyst, himself included, primarily for deceit in their functioning, hypocrisy, sadism, masochism, and financial self-interest (*Diary*, 1988[1933]).

That Ferenczi influenced Klein is evident though she does not accord him much overt recognition. Her concept of splitting was derived from Ferenczi, as theories about splitting of the object were salient in his writings. Further, the hated object, that is, the mother, is also emphasized as a major affective state in his writings (*Diary*) and it is the split between the good and bad object that played such a predominant role in Klein's theories.

Freud, likewise was influenced by Ferenczi's thinking and this emerged in his paper, "Splitting of the Ego in the Process of Defense" (1940[1938]). He highly regarded Ferenczi's paper "Stages in Development of Reality" (1913), and this paper must have influenced his thinking on ego development, ego feeling, the development of the sense of reality, and the ego's differentiation of self from the external world (footnote by Strachey, Vol. II, 66). Perhaps most important was the development of Freud's second drive theory, the Death Instinct, and Ferenczi's advocacy of this concept that received much negative comment. In reading Ferenczi's monograph *Thalassa* (1989), initially published in 1923, from his introduction it was begun during World War I (1914–1918), an assumption can be made that the death instinct germinated from Ferenczi's developing theories. The book also indicated that Ferenczi was concerned with a bio-psychological theory on death and aggression. *Thalassa* resonates with ideas regarding evolution and regression to earliest forms, thus, regression to the inorganic and ultimately to death. What is most interesting is that Jones (Vol. II, 1957) indicated that Freud was interested in working with Ferenczi on Lamarckian theory and its relationship to psychoanalysis. Yet, Jones never made reference to *Thalassa* that certainly showed a cross pollination between Freud and Ferenczi on the death instinct, a curious omission. Was this not also an omission by Freud in his failure to acknowledge Ferenczi's work on the death instinct?

Freud's stressing the importance of the early object relationship to the mother certainly had to influence Ferenczi. In Freud's paper on Leonardo (1910a), he stated: "the accident of his illegitimate birth and the excessive tenderness of his mother had the most decisive influence on the formation of his character and on his later fortune . . . " (135). Eissler (1971) commented that Freud "confirmed—namely that the flowering of genius depends on the early relationship to the mother" (464). This was demonstrated in that he showed how the growing child could be hurt in that relationship and for that reason evolved inhibitions. That Ferenczi in his later writings ignored the role of drives in his explanatory conclusions and focused primarily on the role of the mother, does not negate his earlier drive hypotheses. His belief on the traumas resulting from poor mothering certainly had its source in Freud, but his increasing insistence on a one dimension causative factor helped contribute to his estrangement from Freud.

Abraham

Abraham was born in Bremen, Germany, in 1877 and died in 1925; he came from an old and well-established Jewish family. He was a noted intellectual, steeped in the classics and versed in four languages. Abraham became acquainted with Freud through Blueler while working at Bergholzli in Nov. 1907. This relationship with Freud remained constant and comradely, despite many differences of opinion regarding the political struggles that occurred within the International Psychoanalytic Society. Especially difficult were the differences in attitude regarding Jung. In this, Abraham proved to have had the better judgment. From the beginning, the relationship between Jung and Abraham was conflicted, going back to their days in Bergholzi. Unfortunately, the struggles between Jung and Abraham had undertones of a "conflict between Jung's empathically Christian background (he was a Protestant Pastor's son) and Abraham's Jewish one . . . " (Falzeder and Haynal, 2002). The issues of religion played a role in the early establishment of psychoanalysis. For Freud the concern was that psychoanalysis should not be viewed as a "Jewish enterprise," thus limiting its acceptance by the medical profession and the world. This reasoning probably influenced his selecting Jung as his predecessor, much to the dismay of the Viennese (Jones, 1957, Vol. I). Conflict between Freud and Abraham also developed over Freud's preference for Jung as his successor.

Yet Abraham's devotion to the psychoanalytic movement and his respect for Freud over-rode any disagreement between them; there was never a question of his defection. Under Abraham's auspices, the Berlin Psychoanalytical society was established in 1910. Further, he was largely responsible for establishing the Berlin Training Institute. A tripartite model of training was established consisting of personal analysis, supervision, and formal seminars for all psychoanalytic candidates.

Abraham was recognized as an excellent researcher and had a "masterly understanding of the psychosis" (Falzeder and Haynal, 2002). Though his style is described as somewhat dogmatic and "pugdy," his scientific thinking was influenced by the nosographic tradition of psychiatry and medicine. He followed the behavior and complexes of the patient very closely. Given his style of concretization of the patient's behavior and generalization from the specific, it is possible to describe him as somewhat pedantic. Yet, his contribution to psychoanalytic theory is immense. His work on depression, anxiety, and the psychosis influenced Klein, and continued to have an impact on future generations. What is pertinent in his work was his ability to synthesize the relationship between drives and object relationships. In the paper on "Character–Formation on the Genital Level of the Libido" (1925), he indicated, " . . . early in life the child reacts to the external world purely on the basis of its instincts." As it proceeds up the ladder to the genital level, the child "overcomes egoistic impulses and its narcissism and takes the step toward object love" (408). "In Origins of Libido" (part two, 482), he indicated "and here it is once more to Freud that we owe the first discoveries of importance . . . three phases in the relationship of the individual to his object" (482). That Abraham was clearly concerned with the nature of object relations and their development along with drive phase development emerges in most of his major papers ("A Short Study of the Development of the Libido," 1924a; *The First Pregenital Stages of the Libido*, 1916; Papers on Character Formation; and etc.). In his discussion on the *Origins and Growth of Object Love*, (1924b) he indicated: " . . . we are accustomed to distinguish the sexual aims of the individual from the processes which concern his relations to his sexual object" (481). Of particular interest was the manner by which Abraham adhered to both biology and psychology, that is, instincts and objects. He indicated that psychological development follows along lines similar to "organic growth" and that "Psychoanalysis is constantly finding confirmation in the fact that the individual recapitulates the history of his species in its psychological aspects as well" (498–499).

Abraham's influence on Klein is evident in his thinking on aggression, ambivalence, introjection, and part objects. Though Abraham postulates a pre-ambivalent stage, Klein recognized the role of aggression almost from the inception of life. In this sense, she enlarged on the role of Freud's "Death Drive" and the manner by which this drive evolves in early infancy and its impact on object relations. Though I have taken issue with her early onset of cognitive thinking and the Oedipus conflict, she certainly has posed an important theoretical issue for psychoanalytic theory regarding the "Death Drive." Abraham had stressed the role of sadism beginning in the later oral phase and this would give support to Klein's thinking on aggression at this phase of development. For Abraham, as for Klein, this drive is already directed at the object. In this sense the drive is specific to phase development and not simply a result of the objects behavior. Though Abraham dealt more specifically in case material with the role and attitude of the object, Klein was more focused on drive states and aim. Abraham, in his studies on melancholia, emphasized the role of introjection, the taking in of the object that had to be libidinally abandoned. Abraham stressed that developmentally the "whole object" was recognized only in the genital phase, in contrast to Klein who postulated object recognition very early if not in "utero."

Before leaving Abraham's and Freud's relationship to the annals of Freudian critics, I want to point to an interesting interchange between the two men who were friends, colleagues, and at times adversaries. There was a marked disagreement between Freud and Abraham over a dispute as to who had the legitimate right to produce a film on psychoanalysis, Abraham and Sacks who were approached by a film company, or Bernfeld and Storforer who wanted to produce the film independently. Freud chastises Abraham for undue harshness to Bernfeld and Storforer, causing Storforer to resign from the International (*Letter*, 496F). Abraham challenges Freud on his accusations and reminds Freud that the only differences of opinion between them were always over personalities: "You indulgently overlooked everything that could be challenged in the behavior of the persons concerned, while all the blame—which you subsequently recognized as unjustified was directed against me" (Here he is referring to Jung, and Rank, *Letter*, Oct. 27, 1925, 564).

Freud replied: "It does not have to be the case that you are always right. But should you turn out to be right this time too, nothing will prevent me from once again admitting it. Such differences of opinion can never be avoided, but only quickly overcome" (*Letter*, Nov. 5, 1925, 567). Does this not contradict the myths that Freud was arrogant, authoritarian, and could broach no dissent? Such humanness in both parties and honesty—to fight and reconcile!

Chapter Six

Fairbain

The Reclusive Scot and his Object Theories

Fairbairn may be viewed as having served as the titular head of the British Object Relations School for he provided the theoretical base for much of their theoretical constructs. Grotstein and Rinsley in their book *Fairbairn and the Origins of Object Relations* (1994), asserted that "Fairbairn became the 'voice of the North' in British psychoanalysis," and as along with Ian Soutie, he can be considered "the founder of the school and concept of 'object relations'" (4). He is regarded as a profound thinker whose writings were cogent and generative, and his theoretical influence on Guntrip was extensive.

Fairbairn's physical distance from the center of psychoanalytic discourse and the power structure provided somewhat of a protective shield, yet prevented a more interactive exchange with his contemporary colleagues. It appears that even with Freud who arrived in London by 1938, there is little or no interaction, either physical contact or in writing. Jones (1952) in his introduction *The Psychoanalytic Studies of the Personality,* writes:

> Dr. Fairbairn's position in the field of psychoanalysis is a special one and one of great interest. Living hundreds of miles from his nearest colleagues, whom he seldom meets, has great advantages, and also some disadvantages. The main advantage is that, being subject to no distractions or interference, he has been able to concentrate entirely on his own ideas as they develop from his daily writing experience. This is a situation that conduces to originality, and Dr. Fairbairn's originality is indisputable. On the other hand, it requires very special powers of self-criticism to dispense with the value of discussion with co-workers, who in the nature of things must be able to point out considera-

> tions overlooked by a lonely worker or to modify the risk of any one-side thought (v).

Fairbairn's theories for many years had been in quiet slumber though recently they have been resurrected, and he has been awarded much acclaim for his theories on the object and object relations.

Fairbairn was born in 1889, in Edinburgh, Scotland, and continued to reside and work there through out his life. Fairbairn's early scholarly interest first turned to a study of Divinity and the Classics; he then became interested in medicine and psychiatry. His study of Freud's writings led him to psychoanalysis, and he eventually became a member of the British Society, though he had no formal training in psychoanalysis, either as an analysand or supervisory experience. In a sense, he was an autodidact. Initially, he was interested in Freud's theoretical constructs but by the time Freud arrived in London, Fairbairn was beginning to posit a very different theoretical perspective. He had already begun to question the primacy of Freud's instinct theory and his concepts regarding the Id (Grotstein and Rinsely, 1994).

Fairbairn's compendium of papers written through the years of the late 1920s, 1930s, and 1940s and published in *The Psychoanalytic Studies of the Personality* (1952) indicate the influence of Klein and Abraham whose concepts on object relationships were somewhat more explicit than Freud's. Fairbairn felt that there was a clear distinction between interpersonal relationships and object relationships. The former describing the interaction between normal individuals and the later which give rise to pathological conditions. Fairbairn tended to view the internalization of the object as a result of poor or faulty relationships. A satisfying object relationship with an external object does not require internalization of the object. An ambivalent or unsatisfying relationship results in splitting of "one's attitude about the person," such that the *rejected* part of that person is transformed into the status of an "internal object" (Grotstein and Rinsely, 1994, 5). In Fairbairn's view it is the external person who disappoints and not the internalized object as in Klein's theory that is responsible for the bad object and splitting of the object. His focus is entirely upon the quality of the relationship between subject and object. The good object relationship is not internalized.

Ogden (1983, 1986) viewed Fairbairn's concepts regarding object structures as replacing Freud's (1923) structural model, that of a "metaphor of the mind," with a model in which the mind is conceived of as an "inner world" (referring to Fairbairn, 1952b, 67) in which split-off and repressed parts of the self enter into stable, yet potentially alterable, object relationships with one another. Ogden indicated the "cast of characters (that is sub-organization of the personality) constituting Fairbairn's internal object world is larger than Freud's structural model of Id, Ego, and Superego."

The first paper in this compellation of Fairbairn's writings, "Schizoid Factors in the Personality" (1940) is both a descriptive and theoretical trope, and essentially characterizes the major body of his work. From a theory perspective, Fairbairn whom we know as the "Object Relationist," surprisingly presented a drive approach with implicit underpinning of biology. Though, he has publicly abandon drive theory, it is not possible to avoid recognizing an underlying biological perspective in this paper, and in all his subsequent writings (Ellman, 2003). He presented two parallel developmental lines: the first a libidinal development that has many of the characteristics of Freud's drive theory, that is, libido behaves in a certain systemized fashion. The early oral phase takes the breast as an object, and in this first oral phase, the breast is a part object. The danger to the infant arises from the possibility that his love can destroy the object. At the second oral phase the object has already achieved the status of a whole object, and there is danger of destroying the love object by hate. Though, Fairbairn refers to this theory as an object theory, it certainly has all the characteristics of a drive theory, of libido and aggression. His description of the infant's internal states of love and hate directed to the object is similar to Klein's theories, and like Klein is instinctually driven. His theories of the infant biting, devouring, and subsequent fears of these acts motivate all behavior. That Fairbairn does not refer to these behaviors as instinctual but as libidinal, in no way changes the bio-instinctual quality of the act. What is perhaps most apt is a statement by Fairbairn: "certain views expressed at later stages . . . will be bound to conflict with views expressed at earlier stages . . . " (x).

In his paper, "A Revised Psychopathology of the Psychosis and Psychoneurosis" (1941) he asserted that drive theory no longer provides a valid explanatory theory; thus, "object theory" provided a better explanation of psychic functions. Fairbairn claimed that libido is object seeking not pleasure seeking, and that in classical theory, pleasure seeking is really "a relief of libidinal tension . . . my point is that such tension is inherently the tension of object seeking needs." He further claimed that Freud's "libidinal aims as defined in terms of erotogenic zones-oral-anal and 'so on' are not really aims, but modes of dealing with objects; and the zones in question should properly be regarded not as dictators of aims, but as servants of aims. . . The real libidinal aim is the establishment of satisfactory relationships with objects" (137–138). The difficulty with Fairbairn's enunciation of Freud's description of erotogenic zones is that Freud did not basically consider these zones as aims of libido. Rather, these zones represent the body's particular biological development through which a particular mode of libidinal discharge occurs and subsequently eroticizes these zones. Freud (1922) regarded libido as a "dynamic manifestation of sexuality" and the specific erotogenic zones define the qualitative nature through which satisfaction occurs (132). Freud indicated that the libidinal excitation derives from the nature of the particular zone, and that "Each has furthermore as distinguishable features an object and an aim" (Ibid, 132). Unfortunately, the issue of aim and its various meanings and connotations tends to add confusion to our understanding of aim as a discharge phenomena or aim as directed to a special object. Aim as used by Freud often encompassed both meanings—discharge and object directed. That Fairbairn focused on aim as discharge without recognizing Freud's reference to the object permits him to undermine the degree by which Freud focused upon the object in psychic life. It is true that Fairbairn (1941) acknowledged that Freud did recognize the role of the object, but he claimed that Freud did not develop this sufficiently, and thus this failure represented a loss for psychoanalytic theory.

How Fairbairn characterized his concept of libido is an area of obfuscation. Libido considered as an energic term implies an instinctual force in the psychoanalytic nomenclature, a concept that Fairbairn wants to dispense with, despite the fact that libido is a central concept in all of his writings. In his paper "Endopsychic Structure Considered in Terms of Object Relationships" (1944), he stated:

> I had already become very much impressed by the limitations of "impulse psychology" in general and somewhat skeptical of the explanatory value of instinct in which the instincts are treated as existing per se. . . . What an individual shall do with his "impulses" is clearly a problem of object-relationships. (84).

Therefore despite the centrality of libido to most of his constructs, he denies the import of an instinct (or drive concept) and an energic concept that derives from the drives.

In examining Fairbairn's schema of ego libido as a primary concept and basic to his theory of endopsychic structure, we observe that the ego according to Fairbairn is a "holistic" entity, existing at birth. Fairbairn's ego is a source of libido that seeks out objects, and therefore, is to be viewed as a "dynamic structure." This theory of a "dynamic structure" raises the question of how to characterize Fairbairn's concept of "dynamic?" We may view dynamic from an economic perspective emanating from the drives or/and from a pure mental view as "characterized by constant change" (Oxford Dictionary) without energy. Fairbairn (1946) was critical of Freud's ego concepts as he regarded them as static without energy. He noted that since Freud had indicated that the ego derives from the Id and is therefore without its own source of energy (149), it is an ego that is "empty" of dynamic movement. Interestingly, this statement belies the reality of Freud's concepts, since Freud had later claimed that the ego is the watershed of the drives (though at an earlier point, the Id was seen as the watershed of the drives), and is the source of all energy directed to objects.

Fairbairn appeared to vacillate between a dynamic concept of libido without an energic quantity and a libido concept that relates to attitude. This contradiction is quite apparent from his statement that the infant in the act of sucking at the breast evidences a libidinal attitude.

It is difficult to sort out whether Fairbairn's objects can be understood in terms of energy investment, a dynamic concept, or are they characterized simply by a qualitative attitude.

Fairbairn's theories on narcissism likewise result in some confusion regarding his precepts on libido, attitude, identification, and introjection. He viewed:

> The phenomenon of narcissism, which is one of the most promising characteristics of infantile dependence, is an attitude arising out of identification with the object. Indeed primary narcissism may be simply defined as just such a state of identification with the object, secondary narcissism being a state of identification with an object which is internalized (1941, 48).

Freud characterized energy as invested in the ego as narcissistic libido, and energy invested in the object as object libido. We observe that libidinal investment for Fairbairn takes on qualities of internalization and identification, that is, attitudes, processes that he had also characterized as not operative for good object relations.

Mitchell (1998) considered that Fairbairn like Sullivan was "struggling toward a different way on understanding the nature of human beings as fundamentally social, not drawn into interaction but as embedded in an interactive matrix with others in their natural state" (117). Fairbairn's most "far reaching contribution" was that he was "among the first to intuit that the establishment and maintenance of relationship with others is as fundamental to the nature of the human organism as oxygen-breathing." (118). Mitchell felt that Fairbairn by changing our conception of Freud's pleasure-unpleasure principle added an important understanding to the nature of pleasure seeking which he defined as occurring in the context of object relations, that the dynamic processes of pleasure seeking is the "powerful medium for the establishment and maintenance of connections with others" (120). It is clear that Mitchell regards Fairbairn as the foremost predecessor of Object Relational theory. Yet, one may wonder why he begins a paper "Fairbairn's Object Seeking" (1998) with a detailed discussion of Jay Greenberg's (1991) criticism of Fairbairn regarding the excise of drives from his theoretical constructs. Is he following the dictates of scholarship in presenting opposing opinions or is there some residue of ambivalence in Mitchel's own discarding drive theory? According to Mitchell, Greenberg argued that "all psychoanalytic theories must contain a theory of drive, either explicitly or implicitly," and although Fairbairn presented his object relations theory as an alternative to traditional drive theory, a close reading reveals a hidden drive concept " . . . a kind of crypto-drive theory." (Mitchel, 115–116).

Greenberg believed that Fairbairn substituted Freud's two-drive theory-Eros and Thanatos for a simplistic one-drive system. Fairbairn's belief that objects are sought for the gratification of oral dependency is an example of his one-drive theory. I would concur with Greenberg's evaluation of Fairbairn's inherent drive concepts especially if we question how to understand his use of libido, oral dependency, and his concepts of rage in infancy. These affects cannot be explained solely by the behavior of the maternal object.

Fairbairn's view that the role of the mouth is formed by evolutionary process in regard to breastfeeding is indeed confusing. He stated: "we regard it as oral only because the infant is breast feeding." He criticized Abraham's schema of erotogenic zones as an incorrect understanding of development, as libidinal phases are "really techniques used by the individual in object relationships" (1946, 142–143). It is difficult to comprehend Fairbairn's conceptual framework of a phase—a state of existence—that relates to both biological and psychological development with a concept of technique, defined as "a systematic procedure by which a task is accomplished." (American Heritage dictionary) It is as though Fairbairn is caught between the Scylla and the Charybdis, drives vs. objects, and he is unable to relinquish some aspect of drive theory and thus, must contort the language and the theory.

Fairbairn (1944) dismissed Freud's tri-partite structure of the mind—Id-ego—and superego, and introduced the concept of endopsychic structures that are composed of objects as basic mental structures. These objects remain the paradigm for all future objects representations and object relationships. Though he regarded the object structures as fundamental and asserted that "it is to disturbances in the object-relationships of the developing ego that we must look for the ultimate origin of all psychopathological conditions" (82), he still held to a concept of ego as a structure.

In Fairbairn's schema, we are dealing with two equal structures that constitute mental life, the ego structure, and the object structure (100). The ego structure consists of (1) the central ego (the I), (2) a libidinal ego, and (3) an aggressive, persecutory ego designated as the internal saboteur. Fairbairn indicated that each of these egos is paired off with an object structure. The central ego is the primary, dynamic structure; the libidinal ego (which appears to correspond to Freud's id) is a derivative of the central ego but more infantile; and the internal saboteur (similar to the superego) but "is in no sense conceived as an internal object" . . . is "wholly an ego structure" (106). Fairbairn also conceived that there were many splits in the ego and many egos. While he does not disregard the superego as he had with the Id, he places the superego close to the internal saboteur. Guilt according to his admission has not yet been fully clarified, it appears to merge with anxiety and stem from the actions of the internal saboteur.

Mitchell (1981) stated: "perhaps the greatest weakness of Fairbairn's system is his failure to account for the residues of good object relations and the structuralization of the self on the basis of healthy identification (141). Fairbairn, according to Mitchell leaves one rather confused regarding his concepts on identification and internalization. Identification was viewed as infantile dependence on the object, and both, are two aspects of the same phenomena; internalization refers to taking in the bad object, while the good object remains external. What then characterizes the structure of the ego and ego development is a query raised by Mitchell. Fairbairn indicated that the child's extreme dependence "is reflected in a psychological process of primary identification," and he assigned to this stage, the first stage, as "one of Infantile Dependence, without prejudice to the fact that this dependence is chiefly manifested in an attitude of oral incorporation towards, and an attitude of primary emotional identification with an object" (1945, 145). He contrasts this stage with the "final stage" that reflected a state of "Mature Dependence—'mature dependence' rather than 'independence' since a capacity for relationships necessarily implies dependence of some sort." Further, he indicated:

> What distinguishes mature dependence from infantile dependence is that it is characterized by a capacity on the part of a differentiated individual for co-operative relationships with differentiated objects . . . the realationship is characterized by an absence of primary identification and an absence of incorporation (ibid., 145).

A necessary question in regard to this formulation is what distinguishes the mechanism of identification from incorporation and more significantly, is where do those incorporations and identifications go or become part of, and into which psychic unit? Fairbairn did indicate "This incorporative attitude manifests itself, not only in the ingestion of milk, but also in the psychological internalization of objects, that is, the psychological incorporation of representations of objects into the psychical structure" (146). Representations are of a different theoretical structure than the incorporation of an object, and since Fairbairn has constituted the internal mental world as a structure of various objects it would appear that there is some ambiguity in his use of representation and internalization as the same process. In dispensing with Freud's structural theory his postulated "holistic ego" apparently does not depend upon internalizations or identification with the object. We would assume that structuring of the ego, even Fairbairn's "egos," must depend upon identifications and internalization of the object unless one presupposes an already inherent or phylogenetic structure. Since Faibairn indicated that identifications and incorporations do not constitute the central ego—the "holistic ego," or the libidinal ego, or the internal saboteur, this posses a conundrum. As he has dispensed with the superego as an independent structure, and equated the superego with the ego, the moral ego, we would not expect that identification has a role in this “moral ego.” The sense of a fully formed ego at birth is given further validation by his claim that from beginning libido is "reality oriented," and thus the reality principle precedes the “pleasure principle” and is a dominant force in structuring mental life.

That Fairbairn was an interesting thinker leaves no doubt in the reader’s mind, but that he was subject to multiple obfuscations and contradictions is apparent. That he has fathered a generation of object theorists is certain.

Chapter Seven

Guntrip

A New Movement

Guntrip, the most prominent exponent of Object Relations theory has maintained his reputation not only for his position on "Object" Theory but also, for his portrait of Klein as the originator of "object relations" theory. His advocacy and support of Fairbairn furthered the promotion of this movement within psychoanalysis. With Guntrip's theoretical precepts, we were no longer dealing with shifts in ideology, extensions, or even revisions of Freud's theories, but a development of a new psychological ideology that then fostered an independent political and ideological movement. Guntrip came into prominence after Freud's death, thus his theoretical conflicts were primarily with Anna Freud, Edward Glover, and the Freudians within the British Society.

Guntrip (1961a) stated that his "theme" or goal was:

> *to trace the way in which psycho-analysis has been in process of outgrowing its origins in a neurophysiological and psychobiological philosophy of man, using the instinct concept as the basis of theory, into a truly psychodynamic theory of the personality implying a philosophy of man that takes account of his reality as an individual person. . . .* On its theoretical side, psycho-analysis is the attempt to find out in what terms science can deal with the person in his life as an individual with other persons for that is the problem that has now become inescapable (Preface, 17–18).

He indicated that a "purely 'organic' approach to man is inadequate. . . . When science begins to treat man as an object of investigation, it somehow loses him as a person" (16). Further, "Instinct—theory, in all its forms, ancient and modern has been the major theoretical hindrance to the factual analysis and explanation of human experience and behavior in psychodynamic terms" (1961g, 354).

Let us look at what Freud (1940 [1937]) regarded as the goal of psychoanalysis: "Is it too bold, then, to hope that it must also be possible to submit the dreaded spontaneous illness of mental life to our influence and bring about cure" (172). Freud saw the task of psychoanalysis as a scientific endeavor to understand the operation of the mental organization of the mind, its structure, and the problems that are confronted by the individual in personal development, that not only reflected the role of the drives but also their interaction with the object.

That Guntrip (1961a) viewed the science and goal of psychoanalysis as a means to understand the individual in the context of human relationships, without the impact of drives, does not make him a more humanistic figure than Freud. His approach was influenced by social psychology that developed as an independent field in the early 1900s. Social psychology was concerned not only with group processes and individual interactions *with the milieu*, but also with the individual self as constructed through social relations (Wikipedia). Though Guntrip (1961g) declared that the manner by which individuals "relate themselves to one another" is of importance to sociologists. It is generally agreed that the basic forms of human relationship must be determined by psychological analysis. Not all sociologists have turned to psychological science for this, perhaps because "psychology has not always had much to offer in this respect" (357–358). This statement seems to negate Freud's contributions in *Totem and Taboo* (1913a), *The Future of An Illusion* (1927), and *Civilization and Its Discontents* (1930 [1929]). One may question why this negation of what Freud had to offer to the fields of sociology, social psychology, and anthropology? Further, what motivated Guntrip's denial of Freud's important contributions to the study of object relations, social interactions, and group processes?

Interestingly, we observe another denial of Freud's work but first, preceded by praising him. Guntrip stated: "Freud's first and greatest claim to recognition lies in the fact that he broke into and opened up the unconscious his second must be that he really broke away in principle from the instinct-theory that he never formally repudiated. His super-ego theory laid the foundations of true psychodynamic studies" (1961g, 354). In these remarks, we observe half-truths and misunderstanding; Freud never repudiated or even attempted to obliterate his drive theory, a perplexing distortion by Guntrip.

GUNTRIP: THE MAN AND HIS THEORIES

Guntrip (1901–1975) was born in Scotland. His first course of study was philosophy and theology. He had become a Congregational Minister and his approach to psychoanalysis was "from the religious starting point" (Guntrip, 1961a, 18). He had no formal training as a psychoanalyst and came to the field by the study of Freud's theories. Guntrip was analyzed by Fairbairn and had a second analysis with Winnicott. It was Fairbairn's theories that most influenced him and who seemed most conducive to his own ideological bent. Guntrip was guided by this thinking and believed that Freud's attempt to place psychoanalytic theory within the purview of the natural sciences was mistaken. He indicated that Freud's view of "Scientific Materialism" was more reflective of "faith" than scientific evidence. His concern was that Freud, despite his great genius, had removed psychoanalysis from a humanistic endeavor of understanding and concern for the individual to a theory atomized and abstracted from the person. Thus, it resulted in a cold, abstract, and dehumanized theory.

Guntrip felt that Marjorie Brierley's statements (1951) represented a forward movement for psychoanalysis in her conceptualizing the role of the "active, purposive whole self in its living human relations" (quoted by Guntrip, 1961c, 118), and she replaced what he considered was Freud's impersonal theory of human relationships. He indicated that Brierley worked out a psychoanalytic theory along two lines, one, a "Process Theory," and two, a "Personology" theory (see Guntrip, 1961d). According to Brierley: The word "personology" is borrowed from Smuts as a convenient term to distinguish the science of personality from metapsychology. Smuts wrote:

> The procedure of psychology is largely and necessarily analytical and cannot therefore do justice to Personality in its unique wholeness. For this a new discipline is required, which we have called Personology, and whose task it would be to study Personality as a whole and to trace the laws and phases of its development in the individual life. . . . Personology would study the Personality not as an abstraction or bundle of psychological abstractions, but as a vital organism, as the organic whole . . . (quoted in Guntrip, 118 [Smuts, *Holism and Evolution*, 1926, 293] Brierley, 1951, 124).

Further:

> It is advisable for psychoanalysis to emphasize that they study people not as abstract problems but as more or less well integrated living persons . . . Psychoanalytic personology is a psychology not an anatomy or physiology of personality; it is concerned with subjective experience and the motivation of behavior (1961d, 124–125).

Guntrip (1961d) considered that Freud never made the leap from his early "process" theory to what began to emerge in his post–1920s theories on the ego; he could not encompass, "the dynamic psychology of man as a person" (119). This is a most extraordinary statement in view of Freud's attitude and behavior with patients and colleagues. How do we account for Guntrip's interpretation of Freud's metapsychology, as applied to treatment of the individual, as cold, abstract, and distant and his theories as anti-human? Can we consider that these views reflect both a subjective element and also, perhaps, a not very conscious act of political motivation? King and Steiner (1991) directly alluded to this in *The Freud-Klein Controversies*.

It is noteworthy that perhaps the two leaders of an object relations theory, Fairbairn and Guntrip, both came from theological backgrounds, as did Jung, who broke very early with Freud over the issue of the sexual drive. Instincts and a biological substrate to man's volitional abilities would appear to be at variance with the theology of "free will" and the power of mind that predominates over the soma. The creation of the mythological perception that Freud's theories and treatment methods were "cold" and unfeeling because of his biological axioms, supported their subjective wishes to grant man greater authority over his behavior. Certainly the science of medicine can appear as cold and abstract, yet applied to an individual patient, the doctor is concerned with a human being and his particular symptoms; he is not talking to the body but to the person. Is this not the manner by which Freud worked and, in essence, all psychoanalysts, even those who follow instinct theory?

Guntrip's antagonism to drive theory emerged particularly in his criticism of Freud's papers, *The Ego and the Id* (1923) and *Beyond the Pleasure-Unpleasure Principle* (1920b). To position himself in the arena of the accepted Guntrip (1961c) framed his own ideas in the bastion of Anna Freud as he critiqued Freud with a quote by her (87):

> For it may be said from the earliest years of our science its theory, built up as it was on an empirical basis, was pre-eminently a psychology of the unconscious or as we should say today, of the id. But the definition immediately loses all claim to accuracy when we apply it to psychoanalytic therapy. From the beginning analysis, as a therapeutic method, was concerned with the ego and its aberrations: the investigation of the id and its mode of operation was always only a means to an end. And the end was invariably the same: the corrections of these abnormalities and the restoration of the ego to its integrity (see Anna Freud, 1936, 4).

This primary focus on the ego by A. Freud and later by Hartmann, Kris and Leowenstein, is the scaffolding on which Guntrip (1961c) builds his case for dispensing with the Id as a psychic structure. He will pose the question "Just how endopsychic structural differentiation develops; and whether in spite of individual differences, it produces something like a common basic pattern of mental organization and inner conflict in all human beings. Freud's theory of the Id, ego, and superego boldly affirms that it does and we must trace the evolution of that theory" (89). From Guntrip's analysis of Freud's early drive-conflict theory between the sexual instincts and the ego instincts to his new theory of drive conflict between Eros and Thanatos, he concluded that the Id, as a structure, does not hold up to more extensive scrutiny. The Id, first conceived as the watershed of the drives by Freud, was replaced with his new theoretical construct, the ego, as the source of all libido. This, in essence, showed that the Id was an unnecessary construct as a psychic structure. Therefore, Guntrip believed though Freud did not update his old constructs given his new theories on the drives and increased emphasis on the ego, that in reality a new understanding was required. He further indicated that Freud's basic understanding of an Ego that was primarily conscious—could not also be both repressed and repressing.[1] Guntrip thus postulated the theory that:

> The ego and the instinctual unconscious are both libidinally instinctive and the difference between them really disappears. The difference between the repressed instinctive, sexual unconscious and the repressing conscious and preconscious ego has become unimportant by comparison with the much more fundamental opposition between libidinal and destructive, or life and death instincts, all of which operate primarily in the ego itself, from which they are secondarily turned outwards on to objects. The ego has now become the reservoir of both libido and aggression. It would seem, then, that the instinctive unconscious and the ego are one and the same, while the unconscious in which psychoanalysis is interested—the repressed unconscious—is a secondary thing, originating in the splitting off from the primary ego of that portion of its libidinal and destructive energies which have become turned outwards away from itself on to objects, thereby encountering environmental dangers (1961c, 90).

Guntrip, then concluded that fundamentally, Freud's Ego, Id, and Superego theory is really a theory "of primary ego–splitting" and that a concept of a central ego provides a more comprehensive theory.

Guntrip can then place major focus on the ego as reflective of the entire personality. In fact, he criticized Freud's "self" as an impersonal "it," and Freud's sense of ego as being devoid of energy (93). Guntrip prefers to view the self as a substantive constituency of the "ego," and to use the term "self" for the primary, total, "mental existence," while ego stands for the more restricted conscious "I," that we are familiar with (93). Guntrip's internal world also, consists of the ego's perception of self—valued or devalued, weak or strong, idealized-self or hated-self, and the self's relationship to the internal objects, that is loving or hated objects or persecutory objects. The ego now "is seen to function as a definite powerful person" (99).

The self is also split into an "outer reality ego" conforming to the pressures of the outer environment while the inner reality ego (as a result of the split) responds to the "basic libidinal needs and drives that the child had to repress." He further indicated that "all psychic phenomena whatsoever are, and should be treated as, manifestations of the fundamental psychosomatic unity or basic self which loses its functional unity early by encountering mutually incompatible experiences of its object–world" (93–94). In this sense, he follows Fairbairn's concepts of ego splitting and, thus, the primary focus for both is upon the ego and its interaction with the object world. Splitting replaced structure differentiating and, in essence, the split parts of the ego, become "endopsychic" structures.

Guntrip concurred with Fairbairn's concepts of mental structure and ego organization. He postulated a central ego that is split into a patterned relationship between a libidinal ego, and an exciting object, an anti-libidinal ego, and the rejecting object that he felt represented a more "basic truth" than Freud's tri-partite structure. Further, Guntrip's detailed analyses of Freud's Id and ego provided him with what he believed was a paradigm for extinguishing the superego as a differentiated structure. The superego is a part of the split ego that represents the moral aspects of the ego. Guntrip was also concerned with the role of repression and its relation to ego functions and the unconscious. Since he felt that Freud's ego is not unconscious therefore, in a rather specious argument, Guntrip indicated that "the Freudian 'ego' is by definition not repressed," and thus, not unconscious. Unconscious resistance that Freud claimed occurred in the ego could not be accounted for by the conscious ego. He felt that this inconsistency led Freud to develop the concept of the ego-ideal or superego that would account for the resistance of the repressed unconscious (1961c, 95–96).

Guntrip indicated that Freud did not adequately supply a valid "mechanism of the unconsciousness part of the super-ego," and that his reasoning regarding the development and function of the super-ego left a rather "vague and unclarified dualism" regarding the more conscious aspects of the super-ego. This again became added proof for Guntrip's assertion that Freud's tripartite—structure of the mind was not an effective hypothesis. He further felt that Freud's super-ego had two different qualities that perforce were incompatible, one, a moral factor and, second, "non-moral" that was sadistic and cruel. The moral component was derived from identification with the "Internal Object," "which functions as an ego-ideal." The superego, thus, became superfluous in Guntrip's theory of psychic structure. Though challenging Freud's theoretical postulates, Guntrip did credit "Freud's penetration in concept of the super-ego as parents 'brought in' and 'erected 'within the ego as a 'reinforcement' in the task of repression," as a pioneer effort . . . opening the way to closer analysis" (1961c, 97).

Guntrip was chiefly concerned to show the weakness and irrelevance of Freud's drive theory in structuring of the ego, and further, the inadequacy of his theories in relation to the nature of the unconscious, repression, and resistance. He indicated that Freud's concepts of the Id as "an impersonal structure," and the super-ego as a "dualistic construction" became increasingly quite distant from his own theories on the ego as a whole structure. The mechanisms of splitting and the ego's relationship to the object at birth represented for Guntrip a more coherent psychological ideology. Thus, Fairbairn and Klein in his theoretical lexicon "reveal the true nature of the unconscious as a personal world of object-relations maintained within the psyche and constituting its structural organization. It is an inner world of which we are not directly aware, containing psychically internalized objects with whom infantile parts of the ego are all the time having intensely emotional relationships" (1961g, 359). He indicated that on the basis of Klein and Fairbairn's "object-relations psychology," "it is now possible to give a clearer account of the different fundamental ways in which human beings relate themselves to one another . . . " (1961g, 357).

A NEW LANGUAGE

Guntrip recognized that introducing a new language and a new manner of conceptualizing the psychic apparatus would meet with resistance, as the desire to hold on to the old and familiar is more comfortable. Yet, the question may be appropriately raised whether his claim that the old concepts have become outdated and "stultifying" is valid. New does not necessarily equate with improvement or validity. Unfortunately, there are many limitations to his theories. For example, it is difficult to find an important role for the mechanism of identification in general and specifically with the "good object." The "bad object" appears to play the most significant role in psychic structure. This presents a marked limitation in understanding healthy ego development and even the neurosis. The role and kinds of defenses, aside from projection and introjections, have been narrowed. Thus, sublimation, altruism, displacement, doing and undoing, reversal into its opposite, identification with the aggressor (unless this stands for identification with the bad object), and later phase identifications are barely mentioned in his mental schema. Further, the internal world of ideas, values, creative activity, do not appear as significant to ego or superego development. Perhaps a most glaring omission was his failure to give credence to the place of gender identification and sexual conflicts. Internal conflict, that is intra-psychic conflict, pales before conflicts with the bad object. There is almost no mention of issues of ambivalence regarding identification with the parent of the same or opposite sex.

Further, one is left questioning as to how and what manner Guntrip defines his concepts of libido and aggression since he negates drive theory and energic concepts. Infantilism, in Guntrip's lexicon is defined by the ego's dependent relationship with the internal "bad object." This indeed, appears to be a very narrow conceptualization of infantile dependence. One can easily postulate that excessive dependence on a good object, or good enough-object, may also be responsible for infantilism. From my perspective Freud's tripartite structure of Id, ego, and superego provides a more comprehensive understanding of mental structure, psychic development and functions of the mind. Freud's concept of drives as an energetic force, from an experiential and a logical theoretical postulate, seems to provide greater insights into human behavior and emotions. Guntrip claimed that his theories had a better grasp of the truth than Freud raises a number of philosophical and scientific issues regarding the nature of truth.

NOTE

1. Freud made frequent references to the unconscious aspects of the ego. See introduction (p. 6) to *The Ego and the Id* (1923), also pp. 17–19, 26–27.

Chapter Eight

D. W. Winnicott

The Herald

Winnicott (1896–1971), next to Klein, is perhaps the most renowned of the British School of Psychoanalysis. It is not possible to review psychoanalytic theory without reference to Winnicott. His contributions, then and now, have influenced generations of psychoanalysts, and his postulates regarding the mother-infant dyad echo in the works of Loewald (1978, 1980) and other prominent classical analysts. A member of the Middle Group, he was initially considered a Kleinian, though Klein eventually refused to recognize him as part of her group. Winnicott's supervisory experience had been with Klein; he analyzed her son, and his wife had been her analysand.

Winnicott's first analysis was with Strachey also, a member of the Middle Group. He had had a second analysis with Joan Riviere, a Kleinian who had been analyzed by Freud and Jones. Perhaps it is reductionistic to entertain the idea that Winnicott was a hybrid of both Freud and Klein, unconsciously influenced by his analysts, and ruled by his own mixed identifications. His postulates on projection, introjection, and persecutory anxiety bear Klein's influence, yet some of his instinct theories show adherence to Freud's constructs.

Phillips (1988) indicated, while Winnicott paid tribute to Freud and Klein, he was often in disagreement and critical of both and that "during the 1940s Winnicott evolved a powerful rival developmental theory to both, while including the bits of their work he found useful" (97). Since he was both physically and emotionally closer to Klein, it would seem natural that whatever disagreements he had with her would surface more spontaneously.

Winnicott criticized Klein and the Kleinians for an attitude that was arrogant and implied a privileged access to the truth (see Rodman, 2003). In a letter to Klein, Winnicott (see Rodman, Nov. 1952, 2003) stated:

> Secondly, I feel that corresponding to my wish to say things my way there is something from your end, namely a need to have everything that is new restated in your terms. . . . If you make the stipulation that in the future only your language shall be used for the statement of other people's discoveries then the language becomes a dead language, as it has already become in the Society" (176).

Winnicott's increased separation from Klein and the Kleinians, appeared to give him his creative freedom: "he had located the source of his strength within himself rather than from Klein, whether as herself or as his psychoanalytic mother" (Rodman, 2003, 180). Though Winnicott continued to feel grateful to Klein, he was able to choose his own path. In relation to Freud, "Although Winnicott always deferred to Freud with great and genuine humility, there were instances when he was aware of a conflict, of his own view as different from Freud's . . . he seemed to see himself as the son figure to Freud that Carl Jung had originally been before falling out of favor" (Rodman, 2003, 185).

In spite of Winnicott's differences with Klein and his independent creative ideas, one can observe a marked resemblance to her style in the manner by which he formulated theoretical hypotheses. Rather than present general hypotheses or mental mechanisms, either from a conceptual or developmental perspective, he formulated declarative statements and postulates that have the ring of truth. Since there is no way to refute or prove their accuracy from a scientific or empirical approach, that, from a logical abstract set of principles or hypotheses, one is left with either acceptance or rejection. What is missing in Winnicott's writings can best be elucidated by a statement of Brenner (2006) who indicated that while there is no absolute in science, we are able to establish hypotheses and conclusions that are supported by the data of observation and logical constructs.

To read Winnicott can evoke feelings and thoughts as though reading an essay, an elegiac stream of consciousness that can transcend *one's* own consciousness. As illustrative, reading about illusion and creativity (1971, [1951]), he wrote:

> The mother at the beginning, by an almost 100 per cent adaptation affords the infant the opportunity for the illusion that her breast is part of the infant. It is as it were under the baby's magical control . . . In another language, the breast is created by the infant over and over again out of the infant's capacity to love or (one can say) out of need. . . . The mother places the actual breast just where the infant is ready to create, and at the right moment . . . (11).

In "The True and False Self" (1960), he stated that the True Self "a continuity of being is in health based on psycho-soma growth . . . there is no localization of the mind self, and there is nothing that can be called a mind." In *Playing and Reality* (1971 [1951]) " . . . *play is in fact neither a matter of inner psychic reality nor a matter of external reality* . . . and to his question if play is neither inside nor outside, where is it?" (96).

When he addressed aggression in the infant (1939), we observe the same elegiac quality: "If it is true then that the infant has a vast capacity for destruction it is also true that he has a vast capacity for protecting what he loves from his destructiveness, and the main destruction must always exist in his fantasy. The infant's aim is gratification, peace of mind and body. Gratification brings peace, but the infant perceives that to become gratified he endangers what he loves" (170–171). There is a lovely glide to his writing, but can these ideations really fall under the rubric of a scientific psychological inquiry? Note that these statements refer to the infant in the first few months of life for which there is no available objective findings or measurable testing. His claim that paranoid sensitivity can arise in the first weeks even the first days of life as a result of persecutory fear is another conclusion for which it is difficult to find empirical evidence. This echoes Klein's thinking and style. If there is not good-enough mothering the child, can develop an ego organization capable of using mechanisms of projection and introjection; "if there is not good-enough mothering then the result is chaos rather than 'talion dread' and a splitting of the object into 'good' and 'bad'" (1962b, 177).

WINNICOTT'S ROMANTICISM

Phillips (1988) indicated that according to Winnicott there is no such thing as a baby only a nursing couple; at best, there is no such thing as a mind, only a "psyche-soma" couple (96). The degree of Winnicott's focus upon the mother-child coupling as the primary etiological factor in pathology and in health not only reflects a Wordsworthian Romanticism but even more aptly reflects the Madonna-Child image. There is a sense of religiosity, almost an obsessional aspect to the degree that the mother-child relationship dominates all of his writings. It is as though he was writing a psychoanalytic version of 'Genesis,' the creation of the infant through the mother and the 'going on being' as the absolute creation (Phillips, 1988).

Ellman (2010) noted he "cannot be without the infant mother dyad, wherever else his theorizing might proceed . . . even the instinctual aspect of the infant's development is strongly influenced by maternal care" (375–376). That there is hardly any reference to the role of the father of the child or the husband to the wife (Phillips, 1988), reinforces the metaphor of the Madonna and the child.

Winnicott's reference to the "soul" as part of the internal structure is an unusual stance for a psychoanalyst, and reinforces the religiosity of his psychoanalytic ideology. In *Morals and Education* (1963b), he is concerned with the role of religion. He indicated: "Religions have made much of original sin, but have not at all come round to the idea of original goodness . . . " (94). Though he asserted that individuals collectively have created the idea of God, there is an underlying theological need, "belief in"—man or something. Yet, he also indicated that God is not an adequate substitute for "good-enough mothering."

Winnicott's, Id, Ego, and Self Theories

Winnicott did have a drive theory and gave some credence to instincts. Therefore, in this regard, he differed from Fairbairn and Guntrip. Yet, for Winnicott (1962a]), the Id was secondary to the development of the ego and, thus, the instincts were not prime motivating forces. In his lexicon, the ego preceded the Id and was responsible for the function of Id wishes. The ego initiates object relating: "with good enough mothering at the beginning the baby is not subjected to instinctual gratification except so far as there is ego participation. It is not a question of giving the baby satisfaction as letting the baby find and come to terms with the object (breast, bottle, milk, etc.)" (59–60). In his schema, Id relationships are only meaningful if they happen in a framework of ego-relatedness.

Winnicott's ideas differ from Freud's conceptions of the Id and the ego. In *The Project*, Freud had indicated that a memory image is established in the neuronal system of need gratification, the instinct of hunger, and the object gratifier. When an instinctual need arises, probably the image of the object that gratified is first recalled. In this schema, the Id is the precursor of the ego and cathects the object. Freud stipulated that the ego develops out of the Id matrix. Fundamentally, Winnicott has created a very different psychic structure from Freud. He has created a mother–infant coupling; the infant as the object of the mother, and the mother as the object of the infant's creation that are unified in a symbiotic circle. This process initially constitutes the self or ego. Winnicott asserted that the infant is happily grandiose, for in his discovery of the world he has essentially created it (see Phillips, 1988, 101). Winnicott (1963c) further indicated that by the infant's manner of creating the mother, the self, and the world, this has become the basis of all human creativity. Relating to the object is not simply a matter of maturational process, maturation will depend upon the facilitating environment. "*Instinct-gratification gives the infant a personal experience and does but little to the position of the object*" (181). These statements certainly indicate that though

Winnicott uses drive theory to explicate some aspects of psychic development and object relationships, it is quite secondary to the facilitating environment, that is, the mother-infant relationship. In the paper on *From Dependence Towards Independence* (1963a), he concluded: "maturation process" refers to the evolution of the ego and of the self and includes the whole story of the Id, of instincts and their vicissitudes, and of defenses in the ego relative to instinct" (84–85). This statement would seem to give almost equal weight to the role of the instinct in maturational development, but, clearly, from the over-all reading, the Id, as a structure and source of the drives, are secondary to the infant–mother coupling, and to the ego and self-derivation from this dyad. In regard to the use of the word libido, Winnicott, rarely uses the term; rather, he speaks of eroticism or instinctual love. The reader must assume that eroticism is derived from the concept of libido, the sexual instinct.

Winnicott's thinking on identification can best be understood as a mechanism that both derives from the ego's method of taking in the object and building the inner sense of self and also as an Id process. This primary cathexis to the object is, in his framework, mainly a defense, a mechanism arising from the development of the False Self in order to protect the True Self. He also conceived of a "secret self"—a self that does not wish to be found, the central-self (1963a, 187).

AGGRESSION AND GUILT

Winnicott rejected the concept of aggression as a drive state and, further, disavowed Freud's Death Drive theory. Yet, in the early paper, *Aggression* (1939), he makes reference to "Instinctual aggressiveness . . . soon becomes something that can be mobilized in the service of hate" (170). It is difficult to discern how he conceives of aggression though it would appear that aggression represented a powerful affective emotion in his constructions. At times, he will indicate that aggression is a motoric reaction and a "potential" but there is no indication of the source of this "potential response." What is particularly interesting is the important role that Winnicott will then give to aggression. He indicated that aggression is at the basis of the "primary powerful urge to self realization" (Phillips, 1988, 104). Winnicott viewed aggression as a primary "potential," as the life force, further described as "at moments of being," a very Shavian concept. He also stated "our search for naked aggression through study of the infant has partially failed" (1939, 171). Yet, aggression played a very important role for him in infant development, particularly in its fusion with love. In his paper *Playing and Reality* (1951), he indicated that aggression was primary even before frustration and existed from birth. This would certainly indicate an aggressive drive. Interestingly, he contended that the "word greed conveys more easily than any other the idea of original fusion of love and aggression . . . " (1962b, 171). We observe again the influence of Klein, though, interestingly, he indicated that her views on envy, as Freud's views on the death drive, need to be eliminated from psychoanalytic theory.

Like Klein, Winnicott (1945, 1947) was very concerned with the concepts of reparation, and he conceived that the infant, by "nature," has an understanding that his "ruthless" devouring of the mother and intention to hurt is dangerous. Even the infants giving of "excrement" to the mother is a sign of guilt and, therefore, reparation for the unconscious fantasies of hurting her; "that is to say, to make reparation for greedy attack" (139). Guilt following Klein's theories has its origins very early in the infant's oral phase. It is the result of emerging fantasies of destruction at the mother's breast—the feed.

> Even at the beginning there is fantasy belonging to excitement and the experience of feeding. The fantasy such as it is the ruthless attack on the breast and eventually the mother. There is a very strong aggressive element in the primitive love impulse which is the feeding impulse . . . Breast feeding is the "point of origin of the sense of guilt . . . (the) capacity to hold the moment of concern, where something is owed but payment has not been made" (1954, 143–144).

Winnicott (1939) concluded that these early experiences contribute to feelings of ruthlessness and guilt and result in reparative thinking . . . "back of all play, work, and art is unconscious remorse about harm done in unconscious fantasy, and an unconscious desire to start putting things right" (171). In the paper on "Why Children Play" (1942), he indicated: "aggression can be pleasurable, but it invariably carries with it a real or imagined hurting of someone" (149). Guilt derives from the clashes of "love and hate which is inevitable if loving is to include the instinctual element that belongs to it" (1939, 171). What is confusing in this statement is his reference to the "instinctual element that belongs to it," since Winnicott ultimately rejected the notion of aggression as an instinct. As Ellman (2010) indicated, his reference to aggression as only a "potential for aggression," presented a confusing theory. Perhaps despite the best of intentions, it is difficult to eradicate instinct theory from our psychological discourse. This was true not only for Fairbairn, but also for Winnicott.

THE SUPEREGO

As I have indicated, Winnicott makes very few references to the role of the superego. He addressed the superego primarily in references to Freud and issues dealing with the Oedipal conflicts. Yet, even in this discourse, he rarely discussed the origin of the superego as a structure that developed from identifications with the parental figures and later authority persons. Winnicott, in "Psycho-analysis and the Sense of Guilt" (1958a) stated "Freud used the term superego to name that which is accepted by the ego for use in id-control" (16). He wondered if it was possible to assume that guilt derived from the ego's sense or perception of interior "bad" motivations? He concluded that the study of guilt does not derive from a study of the role of the superego as a component of mental structure but implies for the analyst "a study of individual emotional growth . . . in other words the psychology of the individual" (15). He explained that generally ordinary guilt feeling is thought of as something that results from religious or moral teaching, but in reality, a study of morality will show that it develops naturally in children. "Those who hold the view that morality needs to be inculcated teach small children accordingly, and they forgo the pleasure of watching morality develop naturally in their children who are thriving in a good setting that is provided in a personal and individual way" (15).

Winnicott viewed moral guilt as a result of a natural morality. He was critical of Freud's concepts of the superego, and felt that "Freud deals with human nature in terms of *economics*. In ego-id terms the sense of guilt is very little more than anxiety due to the conflict between love and hate. Guilt-sense implies tolerance of ambivalence" (16). Apparently, Winnicott's sense of the superego develops from its relationship to guilt as this is the only context in which we find any discussion. He noted: "A sense of guilt therefore implies that the ego is coming to terms with the superego. Anxiety had matured into guilt" (18). He does not address the superego as a structure but more as a concept (perhaps some aspect of ego functions), in that "the genesis of guilt is a matter of inner reality" (ibid., 18). Interestingly, Winnicott refers to the "introject" that connotes a "meaningful acceptance." In the early stages of the superego introjects are used to control "id impulses and id products." He further indicated that in the "pre-history of the superego-introjects, they are primitive and subhuman and, gradually, in the infant's development, become 'humanized' . . . " (ibid., 19). This is certainly very different from Freud's concepts of the superego as a structure dependent on ego development and abandoned and introjected objects.

Freud's reference to a phylogenetic basis to the superego may have influenced Winnicott's theories in that he did not regard the superego as a structure but as "something," that appeared to be innate. Also, somewhat illuminating in Winnicott's thinking was the parallel he made between the maturing of the superego in the individual child and the "development of monotheism in early Jewish history" (19). This would appear to confirm my thinking of a religiosity or spiritual quality that underlies much of Winnicott's conceptualizations.

GUILT

Winnicott in his ongoing discussions of the sense of guilt (1958a) concurred with Freud's ideas that guilt resulted from the "clash of love and hate," and he viewed the development of guilt as a healthy developmental process. Though, he initially followed Freud's developmental pattern showing the rise of the superego and guilt as a resolution of the conflicts surrounding the Oedipus complex (18–19), as his thoughts developed, he focused increasingly on the dyadic relationship as the primary source for the development of guilt. The superego and the Oedipus complex was seen by Winnicott as a later development preceded by the infants primary conflicts over love and hate toward the mother. Following Klein, he felt that the depressive position and reparations for destructive impulses toward the mother were the bases for the psychological development of the sense of guilt. Therefore, the dyadic relationship replaced the triadic relationship and the role of the superego, even the term, receded in importance for Winnicott.

It is to be recalled that Klein places superego development at about four months of age, the same time period as the development of the Oedipus complex so that both the dyadic and triadic relationship co-mingle. Winnicott (1958a) placed the origins of the superego at about one year of age. Klein's thinking certainly supported Winnicott's conceptualization of the origins of the superego in the dyadic stage, again stressing the import of the early relationship between infant and mother.

THE SELF

The self-according to Winnicott has an inherent existence almost at birth. He indicated that "this being alive is the early communication of a healthy infant with the mother-figure, and it is as unselfconscious as can be. The non-communicating central self, forever immune from the reality principle, and forever silent" (1963a, 192). In *The Capacity to be Alone* (1958b), he indicated that the sense of "I am" is raw, vulnerable and potentially paranoid (33). Yet, in "Ego Distortion in Terms of True and False Self" (1960), his infant is omnipotent by his very gestures. True, this omnipotence is dependent upon the mother's receptivity; otherwise the infant develops a False Self that is compliant to the environment. To some degree, this is a rather confusing picture. On one hand, we have an omnipotent infant with an already developed self, "I am," who is capable of establishing a False Self as a defense against an unresponsive or partially unresponsive mother who develops traits of compliance and, on the other hand, there is the infant who is vulnerable and in danger of dying if the True Self is betrayed by the False Self. Further, the defense system that the Winnicottian infant is capable of erecting, the nature of phantasies and ego structure, would appear to contradict empirical evidence at this early stage of development.

THE TRANSITIONAL OBJECT AND THE TRUE SELF-FALSE SELF

While I have presented an overview of Winnicott's major theories, it would be helpful to more specifically discuss his two major papers, *The Transitional Object and Transitional Phenomena* (1951, 1959) and "Ego Distortion in Terms of The True and False Self" (1960), papers that deal essentially with the mode of self-realization and the relationship to the object.

The Transitional Object and Transitional Phenomena (1951), on the surface, presented a defined picture of mental life. The simplicity of the concept has a very appealing emotional quality both in style and ideology. Yet, there is much complexity to these ideas. The transitional object represents the 'first not-me experience' for the infant. The infant's initial experience of fist in mouth, finger and thumb sucking, all stimulus to the oral erotic zone that will eventually transition into play with dolls, teddy bear, blanket, or some object. These objects represent the first not-me possession. Winnicott indicated that there is a relationship between the two sets of behavior—the oral stimulating actions of hand and fist, use of the body, and the use of transitional objects—non-instinctual or derived behavior that connect to the mother. He described five types of meaning that this behavior of the "not-me" represents: the nature of the object; the capacity to recognize the object as "not-me"; the place of the object-outside, inside, or at the border; the infants capacity to create, think up, devise, originate and produce an object and the initiation of an affectionate type of object relationship.

Winnicott stated that the transitional object—the not-me—is outside of instinctual processes, therefore not drive related. The question that I raise is what is the causal relationship of this first self–stimulating phase, an aspect of the oral drive to the "not-me" state that he claims are related. Later in the paper, he indicated that the "transitional object is not a mental concept" (9). It is the intermediate space between the mother, the breast and the not-me self. Thus, the "not-me" is not a result of libidinal cathexis to the object, the identification that created the "me" that resulted in the reality perception of the "not-me." The transitional object and phenomena, represent "the intermediate state between a baby's inability and his growing ability to recognize and accept reality" (3). It is the substance of illusion and, in adult life, inherent in art and religion. It is also the "hallmark of madness" if carried to excess. Winnicott gives to illusion a primary state that predates symbolism; it is to illusion that he credits mankind's creative impulses that first derived from the creation of the transitional object.

In the "True and False Self" (1960), it is apparent that the self is superordinate to the ego and, in fact, appears to supersede the ego developmentally. Though the title refers to ego distortion, he begins the paper with a query as to how the False Self arises and what is its function. He also made reference to the fact that the concept of the False Self has been an issue with psychiatry, religion and philosophy, and a challenge to psychoanalysis. His answer to his own question bears more of a relationship to the religio-philosophical vein than to psychoanalytic metapsychology. It is interesting that Winnicott placed infant observation and empirical evidence as secondary to relational factors. He indicated that "the relationship between the patient and the analyst teaches us much more regarding infancy than "direct observation of infants" (141).

This paper, "Ego Distortion in Terms of True and False Self," (1960) has resonated within the psychoanalytic community as an almost philosophical tome. The True Self can develop when the

> good enough mother meets the omnipotence of the infant and to some extent makes sense of it. The mother who is "not good enough is not able to implement the infant's omnipotence . . . fails to meet the infant's gesture. By substituting her own gesture, she fails the infant and is responsible for the development of the False Self (145).

It is important to note that in reference to meeting the infants needs, Winnicott was not addressing "the satisfaction of instincts" (141). Instincts for him are not clearly defined as internal to the infant. The Id need is felt as external "like a clap of thunder" (141). When they (i.e., impulses) become internalized when felt as part of the self, they become an important strengthener to the ego. Here again, we note that the self precedes ego development and the "id-impulse is significant only if it is contained in ego living" (1958b, 33).

Referring again to his 1960 paper on the "True and False Self," he indicated that concerning the Id in relation to the False Self, "relative to this important stage in ontogenetic development belongs to the observation of the infant-to-mother . . . and it does not belong to the theory of early mechanisms of ego-defense organized against Id impulse though of course the two subjects overlap" (144). The False Self develops at the beginning of the infant-mother relationship and is essentially organized "to hide the True Self" (144). What then is the True Self, a question that Winnicott, himself, poses. The True Self begins to have life through the strength given to the infant's weak ego and does not become a living reality except as a result of the mother's repeated success in meeting the infant's spontaneous gesture or sensory hallucination. The True Self "comes from the aliveness of the body tissues and the working of body–functions, including the hearts action and breathing. It is closely linked with the idea of primary process, and is, at the beginning, essentially not reactive to external stimuli, but primary" (148).

Unfortunately, this description of the True-Self does not provide a very detailed picture of its structure, its internal characteristics, or external modus operandi. Winnicott, interestingly, stated that "There is but little point in formulating a True-Self idea except for the purpose of trying to understand the False Self, because it does no more than collect together the details of the experience of aliveness" (ibid., 148). This reply to his own question as to what is the True Self seems a rather shallow response, if not more disturbing by lacking a more conceptual approach to thus comprehend psychic development. Is the self-concept an affective state within the ego defined more by external references to the self or does it encompass perception of drive vicissitudes toward the objects, frustrations, and increase of tension that gives rise to a sense of "I"?

The self, as perceived by Winnicott, appears as some innate quality resembling the biblical "soul." It is there from the beginning, it is the feeling of being alive and does not seem to belong to mental developmental processes deriving from the interaction of instincts, objects, and environment. He will claim that the sense of aliveness can be destroyed or squashed by "the dead object" within the depressive mother.

Self, likewise for Freud, was not a clearly defined concept and he regarded it primarily as interchangeable with the ego, "das Ich." The concept of a mental structure or organization with multiple functions for Freud took precedence over an affective state like "The Self" in Winnicott's lexicon.

The concepts of self have been examined by a number of different theorists. Greenacre (1958) in *Emotional Growth* (Vol. 1) discussed the sense of self as closely related to the development of the sense of identity. The body image, that is at the "core both of the incipient ego and the later self-image," is intrinsic to the development of both the sense of self and the sense of identity. She indicated: "in the first few weeks of life the relationship to the other . . . is probably mediated largely through the touch of skin, and the highly specialized responsiveness of the sucking mouth" (115). While these factors also play a role in Winnicott's infant development, the sense of the self or the True Self is not essentially a developmental self, but an existent, innate self with an already inner perception of what constitutes a True Self. Fenichel (1953) tended to view the self as the narcissistic factor in the ego structure. His general discussion evolved around the development and role of "self regard." This concerns the narcissistic investment of libido in the ego. The development of the self reflected first the development of the ego wherein "narcissistic need and erotic need still coincide completely" (91). In this formulation, drives are a primary condition for the development of the self. I have included these theorists, contemporaries of Winnicott, to show the divide between his constructs and those who have a more structural position.

CONCLUSION

Winnicott remains one of the most read and referred to psychoanalytic writers (Pep Web). His popularity undoubtedly stems from his almost reverential coupling between the mother and the infant. Though his most eminent predecessors, Freud and Klein, had also stressed the importance of the infant-mother relationship, he seems to have won the hearts and minds of many analysts. Perhaps it is the almost exclusive role that he has attached to the mother-infant dyad, a romanticism of love and care, while reducing the influence of drive concepts that have so endeared him to the analytic community.

Recognition must also be given to his deftness as a clinician, his capacity to empathize, and his treatment skills that were exceptional. As an example (1966), in his treatment of a married man conflicted by undercurrent homosexual issues and bi-sexuality, he addressed the problem by stating to the patient "I am listening to a girl. I know perfectly well that you are a man but I am listening to a girl. I am telling this girl: 'You are talking about penis envy.'" After a pause, the patient replied "If I were to tell someone about this girl I would be called mad." Winnicott then responded "'It was not that you told this to anyone: it is I who see this girl and hear a girl talking, when actually there is a man on my couch. The mad person is myself.' The patient said that he now felt sane in a mad environment" (170–173). This capacity to identify and to empathize was particularly apparent in his treatment of psychotic patients (Rodman, 2003). Possibly it was Winnicott's great gift as a therapist that has so endeared him to posterity.

Yet despite his many contributions, there is a large body of contradictory statements that he and many followers have glossed over. To contradict oneself is not a fault; it represents a dialectical process of engaging old formulas with new ideas that then replace the old. It is rather, the failure to evaluate the old in light of new findings and to clarify terms and concepts that is the main problem. For example, what is the nature and development of the "central self" and what is its relation to the ego as a whole; does the pleasure principle impact or influence the central self and how does the sense of reality emerge? For Winnicott (1963c), the sense of reality "arises naturally out of the experience of omnipotence, within the area, that is, of the relationship to subjective objects" (180). Winnicott, certainly recognized the importance and role of pleasure for infant development, but it is as a principle that he disclaimed the pleasure principle.

One cannot leave Winnicott without some comment on the current status in psychoanalysis. That he almost rivals Freud in readership and plays such a prominent role in today's thinking reflects certain aspects of the culture and the personality of analysts. Is the excessive focus on love, nurturing, and the mother, a component of narcissistic individualism and is this increasing in the culture? Are these emphases becoming the dominant mode of thinking in analytic training and treatment? Winnicott stands as a prime example of these trends.

Chapter Nine

Freud-Klein Controversies 1941–1945

To discuss the Freud-Klein Controversies within the British Society is a logical step in this study. These debates provide an understanding of the subsequent mythology that developed regarding the specific theories of Freud and Klein, and as King and Steiner (1991) indicated the differences broke out in "fury" after Freud's death in 1939. What was at stake was the ultimate organization of the Society, training methods, basic theories, and ultimately, issues of power. King (1991) reminded us of the underlying factors in these controversies: "the process of reform and resistance is irretrievably tied to the rise and fall of personal fortune, wider ideological issues, and deep psychological factors at the base of different character types" (2).

A series of meetings was organized by the training committee in order to clarify the theoretical position of both groups. The meetings were organized around specific topics, noted as Memorandums. Scientific papers or a general discussion of various theoretical and technical issues were presented. The attempt was to achieve a modicum of consensus that would consolidate the Society around basic premises of psychoanalytic theory and treatment methodology.

Unfortunately, the aims of the scientific meetings were not achieved. Not only did a tri-part division result within the Society, but also the theoretical differences became solidified. What occurred within the British Psychoanalytic Society portended future conflicts over drive versus object theories. As previously stated in my introduction, the myths that subsequently evolved that Klein was an object theorist and Freud was solely a drive theorist was a falsification of the realities that somehow became embedded in the thinking of future psychoanalysts and Training Institutes. The divisions that resulted made it easier to attack Freudian ideology, that is, drive theory and Freud, himself. That the Controversies dealt with significant scientific issues was evident, but unfortunately, the rancor and discord among the members precluded a more enlightened mode of discussion that could have led to greater understanding of instincts, object-development, phantasy, memory, transference in children, and a host of other significant ideas.

The discord was already evident while Freud and the Viennese analysts were in Austria and Klein was in London. We should probably date the first open conflict of ideas to around 1926–1927. Freud, in 1927, had already taken issue with Klein in relation to her concept of the ego ideal and superego in children. He indicated in a letter to Jones on May 31, 1927, "Mrs. Klein's view of the behavior of the ego-ideal in children seems quite impossible to me and is in contradiction to all my postulates." In a rather conciliative tone regarding disagreements, he stated, "one need not overemphasize the differences between Mrs. Klein and Anna regarding technique and theoretical views" (619).

Klein's stay in Berlin from 1920 until 1926 had already been marked by some disagreement with the members in the society; the differences appeared over Klein's methodology and that of Anna Freud in the treatment of children (Grosskurth, 1987; King and Steiner, 1991). Klein had proposed that the treatment of a child was similar to the treatment of an adult. She had suggested that it was necessary to make interpretations early in the treatment, especially the negative and aggressive feelings. This concept of early interpretation was opposed by some of the German and Viennese members who were influenced by Anna Freud. They felt that the child needed a supportive period and a positive alliance before interpretations should be made, particularly negative affects. Further, differences between Klein and Anna Freud emerged in relation to the role of transference in a child analysis. Anna Freud felt that the child's dependence on the parent militated against our usual connotation of transference.

We may question if the differences in methodology by Klein and Anna Freud were fundamentally the central issue. Freud made this point in a letter to Jones (Sept. 23, 1927) where he stated:

> The difference of opinion between two child analysts regarding the superego development in the child and the technique of analysis are really not so drastic that one could not leave them to historical development, that they have to produce such a premature, passionate, unfair reaction. Is this directed against me because Anna is my daughter? A nice motivation among analysts, who demand that others control their primitive impulses (624).

Freud then confronted Jones directly by questioning his motivations and stated that what is occurring in the British society ". . . has left me with an unpleasant impression and has aroused the need to understand more about the mental processes in your English Society, especially in you" (ibid., 624).

After Abraham's death in 1926, Klein appeared to have lost a protector (King and Steiner, 1991). Therefore, her new residence in London and friendship with Jones gave her a forum to more openly challenge Anna Freud and Freud. She openly criticized Anna Freud as too timid in her analytic approach, while "she (Klein, my insertion) was the true follower" of Freud. She stated that her similarity to Freud could be seen in examining his treatment of little Hans (Klein, 1926, 1927). Can we charitably speculate that there could have been some underlying competition between Klein and Anna that played a role in the "Controversies" as both were child analysts and since this was a frontier field that few analysts, particularly medical analysts, had ventured into, a new continent was yet to be conquered?

The Controversies had all the elements of a Shakespearian drama—a war of words and ideas. On one side were the Freudians—Anna Freud, Dorothy Burlingham, Bertha Lantos, Kate Friedlander, Edward Glover, and the Schmidlebergs (Klein's daughter and son-in-law), Willie and Hedwig Hoffer, and Barbara Low. On the other side were Melanie Klein, Susan Isaacs, Joan Riviere, Fairbairn, Paula Heinman, Donald Winnicott, and John Rickman. The Middle Group, supposedly a more conciliatory group, consisted of Ernest Jones, Michael Balint, W. C. M. Scott, Margorie Brierely, Sylvia Payne, James and Alix Strachey, Ella Sharpe, William Gillespie, John Bowlby, and Adrian and Karin Stephen.

That these differences in technique and theory, the timing of interpretations, the development and role of the superego, and the onset of the Oedipus complex caused such dissention was symptomatic more of personality clashes and power struggles than the issues at hand. King and Steiner (1991) repeatedly reminds us of underlying psychological factors, character issues, and power struggles that emerged in the controversies.

Further, it is possible to consider that much of the support for Klein's ideas and influence on the British Society could have stemmed from displacement of an underlying fear of the new "interlopers," the Continentals who were arriving in large numbers. The analysts who were leaving Vienna, Hungary and Berlin during the late 1920s and 1930s due to the Nazi threat and migrating to Britain posed an economic and political threat. Klein had written to Jones, probably around 1941(Steiner, 1991), that her work suffered after the conflicts that had erupted in 1935 and she complained about his role in the conflicts. She expressed her disappointment with Jones for bringing the Freuds to London as she recognized them as a threat to her power and influence. After all, the Continentals were closer to Freud, the "giant" founder of psychoanalysis, and they could possibly represent greater authority than Klein and the British analysts.

King and Steiner (1991) felt that not only theory and practice were at issue but "power in the psychoanalytic society and its future organization were also at stake" (Grosskurth, preface, 1987). Glover, a former Kleinian, accused the Kleinians of creating an economic enclave wherein referrals were sent to each other, excluding those not within their circle. As King (1991) had indicated, on the overt level, major concerns were couched in scientific differences of opinion but beneath the surface were issues of control as to who should decide questions of training and control analysis, and which individuals and groups held power in the society. Rather surprisingly, King called attention to the fact that there were only two analysts who were Jewish in the original formation of the British society, Barbara Low and David Eder, while the majority of members were Scottish, Welsh, British, and mostly Christians. The Viennese group, were all "Freudians and Jewish." By obvious implication, King felt that religion played some role in the tenor of the conflicts.

Though Klein, herself, was Jewish she was much further removed from her Jewish identity than the Viennese. At one point, she dallied with Catholicism and while married to Arthur Klein, the family joined the Universalist Church (Grosskurth, 1987). Rodman (2003) indicated that the British Society " . . . with its primarily Anglo–Saxon composition, differed from the mostly Jewish societies on the European continent,—"The pragmatic empiricist English character was fundamental to its distinct contribution to psychoanalysis" (5).

Jones, whose role was rather ambiguous in these conflicts and who chaired the Third Extraordinary Business Meeting of the Society (April 15, 1942) indicated: "In my view this problem of scientific difference or, rather, the scientific differences are in themselves not really so important as some members consider. The much more grave and important matters are the personal differences and animosities which lie beyond" (107–108). Dr. Payne also added that "The fear of economic insecurity is important, however because when economic fear is added to difference of scientific outlook all tolerance is likely to disappear and the struggle becomes principally one of power" (140).

Competition and differences were not new to the psychoanalytic movement. We have witnessed the battles with Adler, Stekel, Jung, and Rank that led to a complete break and, with Ferenczi, a rather painful strain in the relationship between him and Freud (Jones, 1957, Vol.III). The battle between the Klenians and the Freudians had a different quality; somewhat like embattled lovers who did not wish to part but who could not get along.

It is not possible, given the nature of this book, to fully explicate the range and depth of the theoretical issues and all the personalities involved in the controversies, but I feel it important to address them at least tangentially in order to understand the political ramifications as to how Klein has been the designated originator of "Object Relations Theory," and Freud was denigrated as being a drive theorist with almost total disregard of his object theories.

Klein though her theories had evolved to regard the onset of the superego, the Oedipus complex, and phantasies regarding the object in the first four months of life and even earlier, did not abandon the signification of sexuality and the death drive. Her beliefs in the role of instincts did not falter throughout her writings, nor did her conceptions regarding the nature of the object change. Rather, she seemed to reinforce Freud's postulates regarding drive states, especially in her agreement with his later developed "Death Drive" theory. Interestingly, the death drive had been received with a great deal of ambivalence among many analysts, particularly Jones, yet it became a cornerstone of her theories (Grosskurth, 1987).

It would be a disservice to both the Kleinians and the Freudians to deny that there were significant theoretical differences between them, but as King and Steiner had indicated, the struggles represented "deeper character and psychological factors than primarily differences of opinion" (2). The multitude of factors that led to the divisions within the society and the particular Freud-Klein Controversies seem to brim with hypotheses.

Jones, though he seemed a close ally to Freud, appeared to have some role in this cleavage. Did he equivocate between both sides solely on the basis of theoretical issues? Could there have been an ulterior motive to his supporting both sides and colluding at the same time with one against the other? In a letter to Klein (1941-quoted in *Controversies*, 229), Jones wrote "the she (Anna) is certainly a tough and indigestible morsel. She has probably gone as far in analysis as she can and has no pioneering originality." We know that Jones, as editor of the *International Journal of Psychoanalysis*, did not publish Anna Freud's paper given in a symposium on the *Technique of Child Analysis* or her earlier pamphlet *Psychoanalysis for Teachers and Parents* though, he published in full the Symposium papers by Klein and the Kleinian child analysts. Freud wrote to Jones (Jones, 1957, Vol III; Grosskurth, 1987) and complained about a "public campaign Jones was supposed to be conducting in England against his daughter Anna, and therefore himself." (Jones, 137). Is it possible to conceive that there could have existed some unconscious ambivalence on Jones's part toward Freud that was re-enacted via the struggle between Anna Freud and Melanie Klein?

As I have already indicated, Freud, not infrequently, had been harsh with Jones and he tended to blame Jones for the conflicts with Rank until he realized his mistake. Freud did regard Jones's sexual behavior with some suspicion and felt that Jones did not forgive Anna for having rejected his suite. Grosskurth (1987) in her biography of Klein felt that the relationship between Freud and Jones "was always to be one of wary fencing." Freud's correspondence with Jung also, gave evidence to Freud's wariness of Jones; he indicated that Jones was "very clever" but he (Freud) was suspicious of the "motives behind the Welshman's interest in psychoanalysis" (155). In a letter to Max Eitingon (1927), Freud wrote,

> I don't find Jones's behavior very puzzling. For a long time, he has been looking for 'conflicts' or fights that hold the temptation to become independent from Europe and to establish his own Anglo-American realm something which he can not very well do before my demise, and he believes that he has found a good opportunity in the partial contradiction between Anna and Mrs. Klein. Perhaps one should add to it a partial anger with Anna dating since 1914, when she refused him (see Young—Bruehl, 1988, f.n.58, ch. 4).

Grosskurth (1987) indicated that Jones continued to act as Klein's bulldog; therefore one can understand Freud's distress about the "English School" when issues of the *International Journal of Psychoanalysis* was filled with articles by Riviere, Isaacs, Searle, and Sharpe, all supporting the theoretical positions of Ernest Jones and Melanie Klein. Still, we must remember that despite the ambivalences that existed between Freud and Jones, the relationship lasted, was enduring and deep. Indeed, so many unconscious motivations and conflicts that we can be at a loss to ferret them all out, and find the ultimate truth. Perhaps the truth lies in the very nature of human beings.

Another factor, though perhaps specious, that may have contributed to the animosity between Freud and Melanie Klein was that her early contributions to the theory of defense had never been fully recognized by the Freudians. Anna Freud's book *The Ego and the Mechanisms of Defense* (1936) was heralded but Klein's work on defenses, for example, on inhibition and its relationship to sublimation in 1921 and 1922, seems to have gone beyond notice. Her contributions and lack of recognition on the nature of these important defenses is singularly notable. It is true, as Glover had indicated, Klein's defense mechanisms seemed to increasingly take on an Id quality rather than a function of the developing Ego. Further the latent rivalry between Anna Freud and Melanie Klein for power or primary recognition in the nascent field of child analysis surely must also have played a role in these struggles. Freud was very protective of Anna and, therefore, felt he had to protect her from both Jones's sexuality and Klein's ambitions. Grosskurth (1987) pondered "who knows what degree of rapport might have been achieved between Klein and Freud had it not been for the hovering presence of Anna?" (189)

It is possible to conceive that a far more contributory factor to the conflicts appeared as a result of Klein's sense of her own greatness. Though she made constant references to Freud in her writings, they have the quality of a reference to some one of the past and that now she had become the true prophet of psychoanalysis. It is not clear if Klein ever had any close relationship or even a cordial interaction with Freud despite their close physical proximity since his arrival in England and their first encounter at the International Congress in Vienna in 1924. There is no evidence of any correspondence.[1] Strange that Joan Reviere, Klein's close disciple and supporter, had numerous communications with Freud, was analyzed by him, and was his first translator. Klein's references to Freud, though seemingly referential to the living founder of psychoanalysis, appeared impersonal; her narcissism could be jarring. Given her increased differences with Freud and her own desire for power and prestige (Glover, 1945; Grosskurth, 1987), this rather grandiose posture could have induced Freud's animosity to both her person and her theories. Klein complained to Jones about his role in the conflicts. She then indicated that her own work was not sufficiently appreciated and that the divisions "did not in any way diminish my conviction about its truth and value . . . " (see, *Freud-Klein Controversies*, 231). Further, she expressed her feelings that the great inspiration she had received from reading Freud's work *Beyond the Pleasure Principle* had enhanced her theories on aggression and later, her theories on depression and the depressive phase. She continued, "I think these findings could not have been unworthy to have been made even by Freud and he would have had the greatness, the strength, the powers to present them to the world" (232).

None of these statements reveal any sense of humility. Had Klein ever attempted to relate directly to Freud, to communicate, or seen herself as a disciple? Or did she see herself as an equal innovator who demanded the same recognition and perhaps more? Winnicott noted (quoted by Steiner, 2001) that Klein and the Kleinians had a too "arrogant attitude that implied a privileged access to truth."

However, as Glover (1945) finally indicated, the differences in personality and struggles for power and control receded against the backdrop of fundamental theoretical differences, differences that created a very different scientific truth and struggle.

BASIC THEORETICAL DIFFERENCES BETWEEN THE FREUDIANS AND THE KLEINIAN—THE MEETINGS

After much hypothesizing regarding the psychological, political, and cultural issues surrounding the Controversies, it is time to examine a number of important theoretical issues that were of valid concern. These differences involved not only theory but also treatment methodology. Perhaps, the most dominant issues revolved around the meaning, onset, and role of "Phantasy" and secondly, the nature and function of "Regression."

A paper by Paula Heimann (see, *The Controversies*, 1941-1945) on "Introjection and Projection" and Klein's paper on "Ego Development" with reference to the depressive position in childhood attempted to clarify terminology and hopefully to develop some consensus, and thus show that Klein's propositions that were considered a deviation from Freudian postulates really extended his thinking. Though Glover would proclaim that Klein had completely changed Freud's metapsychology by her postulates, he accused her of abandoning Freud's developmental drive constructs. At the same time, he felt that she adhered too closely to Freud's theory on the death drive. Interestingly, Klein, according to Roazen (2001), "believed that her own theory followed much more directly and powerfully in Freud's tradition" (1).

Susan Isaacs (see, *The Controversies*, Jan. 27, 1943) was selected to present the Kleinian view on "Phantasies." Her initial paper was a cogent and well-formulated work on the meaning and function of phantasies. Almost as an epilogue to her paper, she positions Kleinian theory as an extension of Freud's theories and that Klein brought "more fully into focus the relationship between earlier and later theories of Freud" (266).

Isaac's theoretical position maintained that Phantasies "were the mental corollary of the psychic representative of instincts.—There is no impulse, no instinctual urge, which is not experienced as (unconscious) phantasy" (277), and these phantasies are present almost at birth. Phantasy according to Isaac expressed the specific content of the urge or feeling, such as, hate, anxiety, fear, and love, and these feelings dominate the child's mind. Thus, when a child feels desire, he experiences this as I want to suck the nipple, bite the breast, and scoop out the mother's body. According to Isaacs these instincts or derivative affects are immediately translated into very specific and concrete behavioral concepts, though she will claim that phantasies are not experienced in words (277). Further, she referred to Freud's views of "the mental expression of instinctual needs," and she thus, believed that this "means not only libidinal desires, but destructive impulses and anxieties also." She indicated that early phantasy has "the most profound influence upon every aspect of early mental development" (267). Phantasies also serve the purpose of "defense mechanisms against anxiety."

The major critique came from Glover and Anna Freud though there were many other interesting and well-defined comments and criticisms. Glover purported that contrary to Isaacs's contention that Freud's views supported her propositions these could not be substantiated. He felt that "Mrs. Isaacs' concept of phantasy is in opposition to Freud's basic concepts of the function of the psychic apparatus" (396). He indicated that Freud's theories of instincts and their vicissitudes are not reconstructions of mental content or interpretations of mental content, but "they are basic operational concepts concerning the psychic apparatus. They describe in dynamic, economic and structural terms those functions of the mind dealing with instinct excitation" (ibid., 396). He made a further distinction between phantasy and the primary role of memory that would precede phantasy formation. This point was also, raised by Marjorie Brierely who had some difficulty with the Kleinian conceptualization of phantasy and would have preferred a different word to describe the process such as "meaning." Thus, she indicated that the "wholesale equation of subjective interpretation, meaning, and psychic content with phantasy go beyond what is required by the fact" (331). Jones, who was in general agreement with most of Isaacs's paper, raised the question of whether phantasy really begins in the first year of life.

Dr. Adrian Stephen felt that Isaacs's paper was really in agreement with Freud's position on phantasy and essentially claimed: "phantasy and impulse to get pleasure are not two separate psychic entities" (362). Dr. Foulkes felt that Isaacs was not correct in her premise that "words stand in the first place for concepts" (363). Words, initially are very concrete and only with development do they achieve an abstract designation.

The major areas of disagreement focused on the onset of phantasies, the timing of translation of instincts from impulses into more specific ideation, and the difference between thoughts and phantasies. The general opinion of the Freudian and Middle Group felt that phantasies, as outlined in Isaacs's paper, could not begin in the first year of life. It was only in the second to third years that phantasy could attain concrete ideation. They further pointed to the difference between hallucinations that were non-verbal perceptions and eidetic states, that is, early precursors of mentation. Therefore, phantasies represented a higher order of mental development and not possible in the first year of life. The Kleinian theories of phantasy involving such highly developed object representations and relationships could not be substantiated by empirical evidence.

There were further disagreements as to the nature of the object in this early period. Anna Freud stated: "Mrs. Klein sees in the first months of life evidence of a wide range of differentiated object relations, partly libidinal and partly aggressive. Freudian theory on the other hand allows at this period only for the crudest rudiments of object relations and sees life governed by the desire for instinct gratification, in which perception of the object is only achieved slowly" (420).

Another major difference concerned the nature of guilt and reparation. These issues revolved around the development and structure of the ego. Anna Freud indicated "---correlation or synthesis of perception and reality testing is achieved in degrees from birth onwards. It would not be accurate to say that this is achieved by the ego, since no ego exists as yet; it is more accurate to say that this synthetic function builds the ego or constitutes the first ego-nucleus" (421).

This contention regarding the level of ego functioning at birth or during the first six months challenged the Kleinian position regarding the reaction of guilt and need for reparation to the object. This also brought into question the nature of superego development in infancy. The differences regarding the age of onset of the various ego functions pointed to fundamental differences regarding the role of maturation as opposed to established innate structures in infancy. Here again, we observe that this brings Klein closer to representing instinct theory rather than a relational theory.

The second area of investigation presented by Dr. Paula Heimann pursued the function of *Introjection and Projection in Early Development.* Her introduction sought to clarify some of the ambiguity that we all struggle with in our terminology. She indicated that terms that are frequently used synonymously such as "identify," "take in," "introject," "establish inside," "incorporate," "internalize," and conversely: "project," "expel," "reject," "externalize," "discharge," still suffer from clouded usage. Heimann defined her use of "introjection" and "projection" "when referring to the mental mechanisms which are modeled on and correspond to the bodily experience of taking in and expelling respectively" (503). She correlated these psychic mechanisms, that is, introjection and projection, with various physical and bodily processes, for example, external stimuli affecting the perceptual systems, eyes, ears, taking in the stimuli and rejecting or expelling some, the process of eating, taking in and spitting out, and defecating. By correlating the psychic mechanisms of introjection and projection with organic functions, Heimann felt that she had established a biological basis and, therefore, a valid hypothesis for the fundamental significance of these mechanisms. In Kleinian theory "introjection" and "projection" were basic theoretical constructs in the investigation of mental development. They are "active at every point and any period of development from early to the 'super-personal function of procreation'" (508).

Heimann claimed that the pattern of taking in the good, keeping out, rejecting, and deflecting the bad is fundamental for life and the structure of the mind (511). All bodily functions are based on instinctual activities, are a paradigm for the mind, and since "these instincts operate in a condition of fusion, each part of the body will partake of both, or will be utilized by both" (514). The relationship to objects will be governed primarily by the two mechanisms, introjection and projection, and since the cathexis to the object exists at birth, these mechanisms are operative with fully developed mentation and purposeful aims.

Though Heimann alludes to the ego, it would appear that the ego as a structure is subordinated by the functions of introjection and projection. From the beginning of life, they continue to assume major importance. Perhaps it is the role of these mechanisms as superordinate to the ego that both Klein and Heimann proposed that influenced Glover's statement that Klein had eliminated Freud's metapsycholgy. Certainly mechanisms that result from ego functions bear a close relationship to the maturation of the ego, but in Klein's psychology, these mechanisms assume "a priori structure" with endowed mental content and an ego quality.

Brierely questioned Heimann's treatment of "perception and by inference, image formation as introjection. Such treatment would seem to equate images with internalized objects" (536). She felt there was a need to differentiate between introjection as a mental mechanism, and the mind that according to Freud was an organization whose primary function was the regulation of instinct tension.

Heimann further supported Klein's theories of narcissism that were in disagreement with Freud. Since the object relationship was already established at birth there was no need for the concept of primary narcissism as the object was already fully cathected. She supported Bernfeld's (1929, 202) concept that "But one need not succumb to the idea that the entire libido is narcissistic even in the grasping period." Further, she indicated " . . . for throughout the auto-erotic phase a part of the libido adheres to objects . . . " (510). Part of this theoretical difficulty and its ambiguity rests with Freud who claimed that the autoerotic phase and the narcissistic phase were without objects.

As I have shown, this claim belies Freud's various statements regarding the presence of object attachment from early infancy and the individual's repeated efforts to refind the infantile object (see my discussion in Chapter 1—Freud). The basic question is the kind of object that existed at this early developmental phase. The Kleinian object is most sophisticated and the infant's phantasies of the object present a very developed cognitive ability. Yet, Freud's claim that the autoerotic phase is without objects is also responsible for the Kleinian claims that the object tie already existed in the autoerotic phase.

As Vorus (2001) has pointed out, the difficulties between the Kleinians and Freudians in defining subjective and objective factors led to heated disagreements as to what is truth. However, perhaps more disconcerting was the belief that each had found their own absolute truth. *The Controversies* certainly highlighted many important theoretical issues and thus, provided the future with a number of unresolved issues to ponder. Unfortunately, new movements developed that denied drives as a biological force and as a basic component in psychological development. Their theoretical frame focused solely on object or self-theories that became the dominant mode of teaching in many analytic institutes. As I have tried to demonstrate the relevancy of object theories were an important component in Freud's theories. It is the integrating of object and drive theory that has plagued the analytic community for many years. It is not "either," "or," but the need to develop a theory that shows how object and drives interweave in every aspect of human development and behavior.

NOTE

1. Klein did utilize the services of Freud's son, Ernest, an architect, to remodel her home in London, a little known fact (Grosskurth, 1987).

Conclusion

To challenge the myths that Freud negated the object or had little regard for its role in psychic development, or that Klein "de novo" originated object-relations theory was the prime objective of this book. A discussion of Freud and Klein, in isolation from their milieu, would have limited our understanding of them as theoreticians and their influence upon the nascent psychoanalytic movement. A view of the cast of characters surrounding them, their theoretical differences, agreements, and personal struggles also provided insight into how theories, seemingly objective, can become fodder in the struggles for power and control.

That Fairbairn and Guntrip could so misread Freud and Klein on the concept and role of objects and instincts in their theories continues to perplex one's understanding. Both men were highly intelligent with great skill and intellect. We may well ponder, what in their emotional core permitted this distortion of the reality? This same question may be asked for their descendants who continue to perpetuate these myths. It is not possible to define Klein as outside the orbit of instinct theory or Freud as alien to the primary role that the object exerts in psychic development. Unfortunately, the schisms that developed between the Freudians and the Kleinians interfered with true collaborative work and important inquiries into mental structures. Klein who made valuable contributions to understanding the object, the function of the death drive, and the role of envy, greed, and guilt was really denied a place in the classical training institutes. Freud's instinct theories have become practically extinct in the plethora of institutes that have arisen outside of the International Psychoanalytic Association (Green, 2000).

I find it difficult to end this book without some reference to the widespread need amongst psychoanalysts from the various psychoanalytic institutes to present Freud in "effigy," as the model to kill. The issue is no longer criticism of various parts of his theories and treatment methodology as a means to continue the exploration of the mind, but the need is to destroy, as though the new cannot exist without the death of the old. It is unfortunate that we cannot look at Freud simply as a creator of a masterful theory who forged an approach to understanding mental functions from a psychological, biological, neurological, and relational perspective. He has been subjected to a range of criticism for what he has not done or done badly, narcissistically, authoritarianism, and so on. It is not possible to read evaluative material on Freud without some blatant or subtle criticism of him.

What is still somewhat astounding is that the need to vilify Freud continues even when new discoveries arise. Ferenczi, who has been re-discovered, and aptly so for he deserves much credit for his theories, is now the subject of a new movement and a number of books. Thus, in reading *Ferenczi And His World* (2012), a very good compendium of articles regarding his place in psychoanalysis and his theories, one is confronted with a consistent array of criticism regarding Freud the man. Ferenc Eros, in defining Ferenczi's work, commented that his differences with Freud is fundamental: "the difference between a humane, philanthropic attitude affirming the analysand's unqualified right to happiness—and a patricentric—authoritarian, deep down misanthropic, 'tolerance'" (46, quoted from Fromm, 2000, 160–161). Hynal (2012) referred to Freud's "detached scientific stance" in contrast to Ferenczi's warmth and humanism, and compared Ferenczi's active treatment to Freud's silence and distance. These remarks cannot be further from the truth (Schwartz, 1998). Freud fed his patient, the "Rat Man," who was hungry; he collected money for "The Wolf Man" as he had lost his fortune during the Russian Revolution. The accounts of Freud's emotional and even personal involvement with patients are quite extensive.

The criticisms regarding Freud's papers on technique, particularly his emphases upon abstinence and neutrality, are somewhat astonishing and suggest that perhaps this critical analytic community with its puerile blinders has missed the essential point. When Freud was writing his papers on technique, 1912–1914, and advocated abstinence, could we in the present not consider for one moment that he was addressing sexual abstinence as, perhaps, a pressing issue in the relationship between analyst and patient? In a politically and adroit manner, he went from the specific to the general and pointed to the difficulties, if not dangers, of breaking the boundaries between patient and analyst. The sexual behavior by many analysts with patients, if not morally questionable, was certainly not helpful for their treatment. Ferenczi was having an affair with the mother of his patient with whom he fell in love. He then took Freud's advice and married the mother. Jones was a womanizer and possibly slept with his patients. Tausk impregnated his patient and Loewenstein was having sex with Marie Bonnaparte while analyzing her son. I am sure the litany can go on. Thus, it is assumed that when one preaches abstinence it generally refers to sex, and not to emotional feelings or a caring attitude. Now, let us look at Freud's concept of neutrality. This has come to connate, in post-modern lexicons, a detached attitude rather than a morally accepting posture-equally distant from the Id, the ego and the superego. Freud advocated understanding not judgment.

Though I have not dealt with the animosity towards Freud by Jung, Adler, and Rank in significant detail, I deem it necessary to make some reference to the issues as I conclude this book. To omit them is to leave open the path to continued criticism of Freud as a narcissist, autocrat, and dictator, the faulty one in the conflicts. It is crucial to understand how leaders and theory can easily be debunked.

Freud (1913a) in *Totem and Taboo*, addressed the issues in pointing to the group or individual's longing for an idealized leader (father) and simultaneously can parallel with the wish to kill the father to become the successor. Martin Schulman (unpublished paper, 2014) referred to the rivalries and jealousies that arise in society as a "culture" of different generations striving for recognition and power. Roazen (2001) indicated that by denouncing Freud as a person it has been possible to dismiss his primary theoretical premises about instincts and their impact on individual and social development. Thus, his disputations with Jung, Adler, Rank, and Klein have been used against him. It is necessary to recognize that Freud could and did tolerate differences. It was only when he devised that these differences in either theory or method would undermine psychoanalytic theory predicated on instincts and resultant affects (Rapaport, 1951) did the disagreements lead to rupture. We tend to forget that a rupture entails at least another in opposition.

The Freud-Jung break had its origins in a fundamental divergence in theory. Freud had anticipated that Jung would become his successor and lead the psychoanalytic movement. He referred to Jung as his "son and heir" (Jones, 1955, Vol. II, 33). Freud actively strove for Jung's presidency of the International Psychoanalytic Association in opposition to his Viennese colleagues who questioned Jung's fidelity and were suspicious of his anti-Semitic feelings. There was also jealousy at what they felt as betrayal of their allegiance to Freud and his turning to the "Gentile" Swiss. Interestingly, Jones recounts an interchange with Jung at the 1913 Congress where Jung was again elected president with fifty-two votes for and twenty-two abstentions. Jones did not vote for Jung who apparently reprimanded him: "He came up to me afterwards, observing that I was one of the dissidents, and with a sour look said: "I thought you were a Christian" (i.e., non-Jew). It sounded an irrelevant remark, but presumably it had some meaning" (Jones, 1955, Vol. II, 102–103).

Jones, Freud's biographer who also was an active participant in these events, does not always pass the litmus test of absolute objectivity, but nonetheless, we must ascribe to him some level of credence. In 1910, when Jung was first elected president of the International Psychoanalytic Association, Jones characterized him as showing two significant flaws, one, he was a rebel, "a heretic in short a 'son' rather than a leader." Secondly, mentally, he had a serious difficulty in that he lacked lucidity in his thinking (Jones, 1955, Vol. II, 33). Yet, the fundamental divide between Jung and Freud existed over a basic theoretical premise. Jung could not accept the role of sexuality in the neurosis nor the idea that libido was an overt expression of the sexual instinct. In two correspondences as cited by Jones (1955, Appendix, Vol. II, 435) between Freud and Jung, he noted that in answer to Jung's plea for using another word for sexual, Freud responded: "-----even if we were not to call the driving force in our broadened conception of sexuality 'Libido' it would still remain the libido and every time we follow it up we should get back to the very thing from which the new nomenclature was supposed to divert us" (1955. Vol. II, April 7, 1907, 436). In another letter to Jung (1955, Vol. II, April 19, 1908, 439), a response to Jung's suggestion that the sexual aetiology of the neurosis was valid only for some cases, he replied:

> I feel a fundamental aversion towards your suggestion that my conclusions are correct, but only for certain cases. That is not very well possible. Entirely or not at all. They are concerned with such fundamental matters that they could not be valid for one set of cases only. Or rather: with such vital characteristics that one could have the right to designate those cases otherwise in which they are absent. As you know, so far no one knows anything about the supposed other kind of hysteria, dementia praecox, etc. (Jones, Vol. II, 1955, 439).

Jones further, indicated that in a visit to Worcester in 1909:

> Jung startled me by saying he found it unnecessary to go into details of unsavory topics with his patients—It was enough to hint at such matters and the patients would understand without plain language being used. It is of interest that Jung himself gave this American visit as the date of his first dissension from Freud's work, though Freud himself did not perceive it until a couple of years later (Jones, 1955, Vol. II, 139).

According to Jones, Jung was concerned about the danger of laying stress on the sexual factors. Jung had stated:

> We should do well not to burst out with the theory of sexuality in the foreground. I have many thoughts about that, especially on the ethical aspect of the question. I believe that in publicly announcing certain things one would saw off the branch on which civilization rests; one undermines the impulse to sublimation. . . . Both with students and with patients I get on further by not making the theme of sexuality prominent (139).

By 1911, Jung had related to Freud that he no longer equated libido with sexuality but rather was extending the term to reflect "general tension" (Jones, 1955, Vol. II, 143).

In turning to the differences with Adler and his final break with Freud and the Vienna Society in 1907, we observe a slightly different situation from the eventual separation from Jung. The Vienna Society was full of strife, pettiness, and struggles for favoritism that would ensure referrals for patients (Jones, 1955, Vol. II). Adler who initially was on cordial terms with Freud became increasingly bitter over Freud's selection of Jung for the presidency of the International Psychoanalytic Association. Though Freud then resigned as president of the Vienna Society and handed the presidency to Adler, this conciliatory move did not really placate Adler. Freud's choice of Jung over the Vienna group was due to political considerations, one might even say opportunism did not resonate well with Adler. His theories began to deviate from Freud's instinct theories, and he focused primarily on aggression that he viewed as arising from a masculine protest. He henceforth considered aggression as the nuclear problem of the neurosis. Aggression was essentially a defensive act against an underlying feminine identification. Adler's theories became a "one sided" explanation, and sexual factors were "reduced to a minimum." Soon he began to view most behavior in terms of "Nietzsche's will to power" (Jones, 1955, Vol. II, 101). All conflict was seen in terms of masculine and feminine protests, and the Oedipus complex was dismissed. It is important to note that Freud took Adler's thinking seriously and in earlier years had thought highly of his intellectual acumen.

Further, to show a un-oppositional Freud (1924) to new ideas, he wrote to the Committee (the group of analysts in Vienna around Freud) on the nature of Otto Rank's theories on the birth trauma, "I do not hesitate to say that I regard this work as highly significant, that it has given me much to think about, and that I have not yet come to a definitive judgment about it . . . for the time being I must leave the matter open" (Jones, 1957, Vol. III, 61–62). He further requested of the other analysts "not to form too quickly a judgment, least of all a disapproving one . . . " (ibid., 62–63).

As I had indicated in the chapter on Klein, there existed a similar conciliatory attitude toward her. We observe an open-minded pattern in his responses though Freud differed from Klein on a number of issues. A letter from Freud to Jones (Jones, 1957, Vol. III) clearly, indicated Freud's ability to tolerate differences and to enjoin them wherever possible. Thus, he wrote to Jones in 1927:

> I do not estimate our theoretical differences of opinion as slight, but so long as there is no bad feeling behind them they can have no troublesome results. I can say definitely that we in Vienna have not infused any ill will into the contradiction, and your amiableness has prepared the way in which Melanie Klein

> erred in this respect toward Anna. It is true I am of the opinion that your Society has followed Frau Klein on a wrong path, but the sphere from which she has drawn her observations is foreign to me so that I have no right to any fixed conviction (197–198).

This is a rather conciliatory statement from a man supposedly narcissistic, authoritarian, and who could not suffer differences. Another quite touching communication between Freud and Ferenczi (Jones, 1957, Vol. III, Jan. 22, 1924) will further illustrate that Freud could uphold the value of a scientific ethic even in the face of differences. He wrote:

> That as for your endeavor to remain in complete agreement, I treasure it as an expression of your friendship, but find this aim neither necessary or easily attainable. I know that I am not very accessible and find it hard to assimilate alien thoughts that do not quite lie in my path. It takes a time before I can make a judgment about them. . . . If you were to wait so long each time there would be an end to your productivity. That won't do at all. . . . Why shouldn't you therefore have the right to try if things won't work in another way from what I had thought. (57).

In presenting these statements about Freud and his relationships with Jung, Adler, Rank, Ferenczi, and Klein, it is possible to acquire a very different picture of Freud, the theorist, the leader of a new movement, and the man. I wanted to expunge the verdict of Freud as the autocrat who could not tolerate differences and the narcissist that needed total allegiance. That Freud's writings have a great deal to teach us is incontestable. Sociology and Anthropology, likewise, have much to gain from his work, especially, *Totem and Taboo*, *The Future of an Illusion*, and *Civilization and Its Discontents*.

I recognize that though I have provided a far more detailed discussion to Freud the person, his theories, and general thinking than I have to Klein's thinking, this despite the title, *The Mythology Surrounding Freud and Klein*. The juxtaposition of them in tandem was important in order to expose the myth that Klein was the originator of "Object Relations Theory" and that Freud was solely a drive theorist. Klein has been used to discredit Freud, and her theories have been distorted. She was the impetus for establishing the British Kleinian group of psychoanalysis, and her theories were an amalgam of drives, drive states, and drive-objects that put her closer to Freud than the current "Object Theorists."

To reconsider Klein's contributions is a prerequisite for the study of psychoanalysis. She made important contributions to the theory and, in particular, on envy and greed. Her stress of the death drive and its impact on infant development has not received sufficient attention. Though she regarded the aggressive instinct as the primary exponent of the "Death Drive," she recognized that the death drive had important implications for psychic development in the earliest stages of infancy. Despite her signification of elaborate thinking and detailed phantasy formation in the infant, she did raise some issues (almost neglected by theorists) regarding the interaction between Eros and Thanatos. The emotional effects and subsequent mentation in the infant and young child bear the imprint of these two drives, and though different in time sequence from Freud's schema, nevertheless require further exploration and examination.

To give credence to new and divergent theories, to explore new frontiers does not necessitate the bludgeoning of the old. Further, despite the decline of the neurotic patient and the increase of the narcissistic patient, the idea that instincts are a theoretical concern of the past and even then had little bearing on mental structure, does a gross injustice to psychoanalytic theory, and creates a treatment devoid of real depth. The psychic mind is a constituency of both drives and objects and requires a stance that considers how and in what manner in each developmental phase they interact. Diagnosis explains psychic structure, strengths, and weaknesses in the manner by which object identifications, object constancy, and the modulation and sublimation of the drives have either succeeded or failed in building adequate self and object representations. These representations ultimately inform us regarding the strength and functions of Id, Ego, and Superego. The treatment of the narcissistic or more disturbed patient demands of the analyst skills to treat the person not the theory.

Appendix

Michael Balint

The Un-Remembered

Balint was born in Hungary in 1896. He was analyzed by Ferenczi and was a member of the Budapest society. He emigrated to England prior to World War II where he became a member of the British Psychoanalytic Society. He was a none too recognized figure in this glossary of eminent analysts who were actively engaged in the "Controversies" (1941–1945) over drive and object theory. It is my opinion that Balint made important contributions to psychoanalytic theory, especially by his attempts to harmonize drive and object theory in a more integrated manner. Balint, who as part of the middle group which maintained a neutral position between the Freudians and the Kleinians, provided an interesting bridge between Freud's drive theories and the object theorists Fairbairn, Guntrip, and others.

Balint, through his close association with Ferenczi and appreciation of his work, was able to expound upon his object theories that thus brought Ferenczi into greater prominence within the analytic orbit of the object theorists. Ferenczi's theories on the object had a history prior to Fairbairn, Guntrip, and Klein. Further, Balint attempted to provide a synthesis regarding Ferenczi's earlier drive theories with his later theories on the mother-child relationship. Though Balint accepted much of Freud's theories and attempted to harmonize drive and object postulates in his own work, there were differences between the two theoretical positions. The mother-child dyad was of particular interest for him. He continued to explore this aspect of Ferenczi's work, even some of the more questionable parts of Ferenczi's theories and treatment methods in order to understand their possible validity for future psychoanalytic work. Balint's own writings are quite interesting, particularly his theories on *The Basic Fault* and the pre-oedipal aspects of the mother-child dyad. Significantly, he addressed the idea of a "two-person psychology" within the three-person constellation of the oedipal, in early development, and also its important role in the analytic relationship (1968, 132). Unfortunately, neither the British, American Object-Relationists, nor the more classical analysts had accorded Balint sufficient recognition for his attempts at integrating drives and object in psychic development.

A possible explanation for the neglect and bypassing of many of his theories may be that Balint who had stressed the role of the object in infant development did not reject drive theory. Though he modified certain aspects of Freud's drive theory, he gave credence to the role of instincts and their role both in normal development and in pathogenic conflicts. Balint recognized this neglect by both the mainstream classical analysts and those whom he referred to as the "fringe element" in psychoanalysis (153–155). The more classical psychoanalysts' failure to recognize the value of his work probably had more to do with his role as an amender on Freud's theories both on drives and objects, rather than complete acceptance. His focus on the nature of the object relations in the transference between the patient and the analyst brought into sharp relief the role that the instincts, love and hate, played both in psychic development and in the treatment. Balint described the transference situation as one of an interdependent role with the analyst who is able to ferret out the repressed. He stressed the object relationship within the analytic setting that enables the "relief of repression of instinctual wishes." Therefore, the patient is able to experience the forbidden wishes in a safe environment (132). A second reason for why Balint had not been embraced by the Relational, the Intersubjective, and the Post-Modernist analysts was his failure to characterize Freud as the cold, authoritarian leader and anti-humanist analyst (Fromm, 1963).

Balint's discussion of the estrangement between Freud and Ferenczi pointed to the tragedy of the situation. He indicated that "Ferenczi, because of his own uncertainty could not make use of Freud's well-meant and well-founded criticisms; he saw in them only a lack of understanding." Balint felt that the "disagreement between Freud and Ferenczi acted as a trauma on the psychoanalytic world" (152). These statements from a man who admired Ferenczi, was analyzed by him, and even continued Ferenczi's experiments of active therapy, indicated the degree of objectivity that is possible even with differences and disagreements.

Balint's understanding of Freud's reluctance to treat regressed patients and Freud's claim that they were un-analyzable, demonstrates a thoughtful, sympathetic approach rather than a dismissive, pejorative attitude that has become de reguer of post-modernism. He placed Freud in his historical context and examined the roots of his theoretical understandings, his early work with regressed patients, Breuer's work with Anna O., and Freud's own work with hysteria. It was this early work that led Freud to his negative conclusions regarding the analyzability of the more regressed patients. Balint indicated:

> It is no wonder that when he saw Ferenczi, for whom he had so much affection and whom he held in such high esteem, slipping away into the same morass from which he (Freud) could escape only by a supreme effort, he could not help becoming alarmed, critical and—what is very rare indeed for Freud—somewhat insensitive. He saw "clearly and correctly, the dangers that Ferenczi was courting, but could not recognize, nor appreciate, the possibilities of a new and important development both in our technique and our theory" (150).

This empathy for Freud merits much praise, as it comes from a man who worked closely with Ferenczi and who supported many of his theories. Balint himself recognized the failures in Ferenczi's active therapy and yet, he continued the experiment with the more disturbed and regressed patients. Balint believed that it was possible to develop techniques that would prove useful and productive, both for curative methods for the more regressed patients and theoretical understanding.

Balint was not interested in going outside the bounds of classical, that is Freud's theories. Rather, his interest was in expanding what he considered to be the basic constructs of psychoanalysis. Thus, he maintained a positive attitude toward the instincts and widened Freud's early concepts of the object and object relations. He indicated that "According to my theory, the individual is born in a state of intense relatedness to his environment, both biologically and libidinal. Prior to birth, self and environment are harmoniously 'mixed up'; in fact they interpenetrate each other. In this world, as has been mentioned, there are as yet no objects, only limitless substances or expanses" (*The Basic Fault*, 1968, 67). Though the drives exist as an inherent biological state, Balint posited that the environment as responded to *in utero* had become an inherent aspect of ego development. He did not claim that the drives seek objects, as do the object relationists, rather the environment is experienced; it has already been incorporated by the fetus. The neural patterning was inherent in mental processing for response to the environment. He stated:

> Birth is a trauma that upsets this equilibrium by changing the environment radically and enforces—under the real threat of death—a new form of adaptation. This starts off, at any rate considerably accelerates, the separation between individual and environment. Objects, including the ego begin to emerge from the mix-up of substances and from the breaking up of the harmony of the limitless expanses. The Objects have—in contrast to the friendlier substances—firm contours and sharp boundaries, which henceforth must be recognized and respected. Libido is no longer in a homogeneous flux from the id to the environment; under the influence of the emerging objects, concentrations and rarefactions appear in its flow" (ibid., 67).

Balint accepted Freud's libidinal theory in total. Yet, in regard to the aggressive drive, it would appear that he viewed aggression as reactive to frustration ("On Love and Hate," 1951, 71). He was critical of Freud's theories of primary and secondary narcissism (*Primary Object Love*, 1937 [1952]), and attempted to prove that all narcissism is of a secondary character. Since primary love of the object described the infantile condition, a state in which self and object are considered as one unit, libido is invested in this unified self-object. Therefore, libido, once there is a separation between self and object, flows back solely to the self and is, therefore, secondary narcissism. It would seem that Balint's distinction between secondary and primary narcissism is necessary for his theoretical construct of oneness between fetus and object beginning in inter-utero space. In this construct, libido is initially invested in the dual unity of self and object, and only at separation does the libido invest only the self with libido. This postulate would also give credence to Winnicott's and Loewald's ideas that one cannot consider the baby without the mother. Though Balint emphasized the concept of "primary love," a state that characterizes the relationship between the mother and the baby beginning in utero.

Balint (1968) accepted Freud's theories of the Oedipus complex, recognizing it as a universal phenomenon in both normal and pathological development. Regarding the more recent developments in psychoanalytic theory on the place of pre-oedipal pathology, he introduced a new terminology that interestingly supported the relational theories. He felt that the term basic fault would better describe the difficulties in ego structure that could also apply to Oedipal and pre-oedipal difficulties (11–17). *The Basic Fault* involved a disturbance in the two-person relationship that preceded the three-person triangular relationships of later development. He indicated that this "two person relationship is of a particular nature, entirely different from the well known human relationships of the Oedipal period." Further, he indicated that these earlier relationships differed significantly in the understanding of words and did not involve "conflict." Therefore, he did not subscribe to the "Death Instinct" and its role in creating ambivalence and conflict as purported by the Kleinians. This early free conflict state for Balint represented a period when the need for safety and sympatica from the object were paramount. If these were missing from the caretaker's responses to the infant, then in its wake a fault developed in the ego structure. This basic ego fault required a different level of response from the analyst. Balint was concerned that our common language of interpretation could not emotionally reach this population and therefore, a different level of attunement was required (16, 19). This concept of the basic fault has not found its way into the psychoanalytic lexicon perhaps due to its strangeness and its distance from the already accepted oedipal and pre-oedipal terminology. Yet, the idea has merit and is a parallel concept with the meanings inherent in pre-oedipal constructs. The "fault," according to Balint, is neither vertical nor horizontal, and thus the pathology also exists in the sphere of the oedipal constellation.

Though Balint accepted the libidinal instinct as predominant in psychic development, he took issue with Freud's delineation of the source of libido. He pointed to contradictory statements by Freud that the libido initially derived from the Id (the Id as the great reservoir of libido, Standard Edition, Vol. 19, 30), and later indicated that the Ego was the watershed of the drives (quoted by Balint, 1968, 41). This issue concerned Balint as it was related to his own attempts to show that narcissism was essentially secondary narcissism. The first cathexis was the attachment to the object in a fused state, and therefore, libido that resided in the ego was the result of cathexis withdrawn from the primary love object to the ego. Balint felt that Freud did not resolve the contradictory positions as to the original source of libido, that is, either in the Id or Ego. This was essentially due to the fact that Freud was governed by observable facts rather than reified theory. He indicated: "Freud's unwillingness to give up or modify clinical observations for the sake of a tidy theory. The reason why he always and invariably returned to the cathexis of the ego by libido when he was talking about narcissism, is simply that this is *what can be observed*; everything else is speculation, plausible or false, but not observable clinical fact" (45).

Balint, in spite of his criticisms regarding contradictions in some concepts regarding the Ego and Id on narcissism and what to him were also insufficient attention to the role of the object both in Freud's theoretical and clinical writings, continued to follow Freud's drive theory and biological perspective. He did not regard Freud as the awful authoritarian who could tolerate no dissidence, but regarded Freud as a kind and sensitive man and regrettably placed Balint beyond the ken of the new establishment of the object theorists, who themselves unfortunately seem to demand total loyalty (Rangel, 2002).

References

Abraham, K. (1968)[1911]. "Notes on the psycho-analytic Investigation and Treatment of Manic –depressive Insanity and Allied conditions." In *The Selected Papers of Karl Abraham*, 137-156. London, England: Hogarth Press, LTD And the Institute for Psychoanalysis.

———. (1968)[1916]. "The First Pregenital Stage of the Libido." In *The Selected Papers of Karl Abraham*, 248-279. London, England: Hogarth Press, LTD And the Institute for Psychoanalysis.

———. (1968)[1924a]. "A Short Study of the Development Of The Libido Viewed In The Light of Mental Disorders." In *The Selected Papers of Karl Abraham*, 418-469. London, England: Hogarth Press LTD And The Institute for Psychoanalysis.

———. (1968)[1924b]. "Origins And Growth of Object Love." In *The Selected Papers of Karl Abraham*, 480-516. London, England: Hogarth Press LTD And The Institute of Psychoanalysis.

———. (1968)[1925]. "Character Formation on the Genital Level of the Libido." In *The Selected Papers of Karl Abraham*, 407-417. London, England: Hogarth Press LTD And The Institute of Psychoanalysis.

Aron, L. 1995. "The Internalized Primal Scene." *Psychoanalytic Dialogues* 5:195-237.

Balint, M. 1952[1937]. "Early Developmental States of the Ego: Primary Object - Love." In *Primary Love and Psycho-Analytic Technique*, 90-108. London: Tavistock Publications.

———. 1952 [1951]. "On Love and Hate." In *Primary Love and Psycho-Analytic Technique*, 141-138. London: Karnac Books Ltd.

———. 1968. "The Basic Fault: Therapeutic Aspects of Regression." New York: Brunnel/ Mazel.

Bernfeld, S. 1929. "The Psychology of the Infant." London: Routledge & Kegan Paul.

Blum, H. 2007. "Little Hans Revisited: A Centennial Review and Reconstruction." *Journal of The American Psychoanalytic Association*, Vol 3, 749-766.

———. 2011. "Introduction." *Psychoanalytic Review*. 87:859-861.

Brenner, C. 1982. "The Mind In Conflict." New York: International Universities Press Inc.

———. 2006. "Psychoanalysis or Mind And Meaning." New York: The Psychoanalytic Quarterly, Inc.

Breuer, J. & Freud, S. 1893-1895. London: Hogarth Press and The Institute of Psychoanalysis, Studies On Hysteria. S.E., 2.

Brierley, M. 1951. "Trends in Psychoanalysis." London: Hogarth.

Busch, F. 1999. "Rethinking Clinical Technique." Northvale, New Jersey: Jason Aronson Inc.

Charcot, J.M. 1886-1890. Oeuvres Completes (9 vols.), Paris, France.

Chusid, J. 2007. "Little Hans 'Analyzed' in The Twentieth Century." *Journal of The American Psychoanalytic Association*. Vol. 55, 749-767.

Compton, A. 1981. "On the Psychoanalytic Theory of Instinctual Drives." *Psychoanalytic Quarterly*, 50:190-237.
———. 1983a. "The Current Status of the Psychoanalytic Theory of Instinctual Drives. 1: Drive concept, classification, and development." *Psychoanalytic Quarterly*, 52:364-401.
———. 1983b. "The Current Status of the Psychoanalytic Theory of Instinctual drives –11: the Relation of the Drive Concept to Structures, Regulatory Principles and Object." *Psychoanalytic Quarterly*, 52:402-426.
———. 1985. "The Development of the Drive Concept in Freud's work: 1905 –1915." *Journal of American Psychoanalytic Association*, 33:93–115.
———. 1986. "Freud: Objects and Structure." *Journal of American Psychoanalytic Association*, 34:56:590.
Curtis,H. C. 1985. "Clinical Perspectives In Self Psychology." *Psychoanalytic Quarterly* 54:339-378.
Darwin, C. 1871. "The Descent of Man, and Selection in Relation to Sex." (2 vols.) London: England.
Deutsch, F. 1957. A Footnote to Freud's "Fragment of the Analysis of a Case of Hysteria." *Psychoanalytic Quarterly* 16:159-167.
Dupont, J.D. 1955[1988]. *The Clinical Diary of Sándor Ferenczi*, edited by Judith Dupont, Harvard University Press: Cambridge Press, 1988.
———. Feb. 2, 1932a. "A Dilemna of Mutual Analysis," 28-29.
———. Feb. 14, 1932b. "On the Acceptance of Unpleasure," 31-34.
———. Feb. 16, 1932c. "Limitations of Mutal Analysis," 34-37.
———. Feb. 21, 1932d. "Fragmentation," 38-40.
———. May 10, 1932e. "Traumatic Self Strangulation," 102-106.
———. July 30, 1932f. "Literal" Repetition Endlessly Repeated and No Recollection, 179-184.
———. Aug. 4, 1932g. "Personal causes for the erroneous development of psychanalysis. 184-187.
Eissler, K. 1971. "Talent and Genius." New York: World Publishing.
Ellis, H. 1898. "Hysteria in relation to the sexual emotions." *The Alienist and Neurologist*,19.
Ellman, S. 2010. "Winnicott: In Search of the Real." In *When Theories Touch: A Historical and Theoretical Integration of Psychoanalytic Thought*. 359-412. London: Karnack Books Ltd.
Eros, F. 2004. "The Ferenczi Cult: Its Historical and Political Roots." *International Forum of Psychoanalysis*, Vol.13, 122-128.
———. 2012. "Some Social and Political issues Related to Ferenczi and the Hungarian School." In *Ferenczi and His World: Rekindling The Spirit of the Budapest School*, 39-54. London, England: Karnac.
Fairbairn, W.R. 1952[1940]. "Schizoid Factors In the Personality." In *Psychoanalytic Studies Of The Personality*, 3-27, London: Henley and Boston: Routledge & Kegan Paul.
———. 1952a[1941]. "A Revised Psychopathology of the Psychosis and the Psychoneurosis." In *Psychoanalytic Studies of the Personality*, 28-58. London: Henley, Boston: Routledge, Kegan, and Paul.
———. 1952b [1943]. "The Repression And The Return Of Bad Objects" (With Reference To 'The War Neuroses'). In *Psychoanalytic Studies Of The Personality*, 59-81. London: Henley, and Boston: Routledge & Kegan Paul.
———. 1952c [1944]. "Endopsychic Structure Considered In Terms Of Object-Relationships." In *Psychoanalytic Studies Of The Personality*, 82-136. London: Henley, and Boston: Routledge & Kegan Paul.
———. 1952d [1946]. "Object – Relationships and Dynamic Structure." In *Psychoanalytic Studies Of The Personality*, 137-151. London: Henley, and Boston: Routledge & Kegan Paul.
Falzeder, E.; Brabant, E.; and Giampieri-Deutsch, P. (Editors) 1996. "The Correspondence of Sigmund Freud and Sándor Ferenczi," Vol. 2, 1914-1919. London/New York: Karnac.
Falzeder, E. & Haynal A. (Editors) 2002. "Introduction: To The Complete Correspondence of Sigmund Freud and Karl Abraham," 1907-1925. London/New York: Karnac.
———. 2002, 496F.

———. 2002[1925] October 27, 564.
———. 2002[1925] November 5, 567.
Fechner, G. 1873. Einige Ideen zur Schopfungs- und Entwickelungsgeschichte der organnismen. Leipzig: Breitkof und Hartel.
Fenichel, O.1953a. "Some Infantile Sexual Theories Not Hitherto Described." In *The Collected Papers Of Otto Fenichel*, 1st series, 117-122. New York: David Lewis, Inc.
———. 1953b. "A Critique of the Death Instinct." In *The Collected Papers of Otto Fenichel*, 1st. series, 137-151. New York: Norton.
Ferenczi, S. 1913. "Stages in the Development of the Sense of Reality." In *Sex In Psychoanalysis, 1950*, Vol. I, 213-239. New York: Basic Books.
———. 1922. "Freud's 'Group Psychology and The Analysis of the Ego.'" In *The Selected Papers of Sándor Ferenczi: Problems and Methods of Psychoanalysis*, edited by M. Balint, 1955, Vol. 111, 371-376. New York: Basic Books.
———. 1926. "To Sigmund Freud On His Seventieth Birthday." In: *Final Contributions To the Problems & Methods Of Psychoanalysis, Vol. III*, edited by M. Balint, 1955, 371-376. New York: Basic Books.
———. 1933. "Confusion of Tongues Between Adults and the Child." In *Final Contributions To The Problems and Methods of Psychoanalysis*, edited by M. Balint, 1955, 156-167. New York: Basic Books.
———. 1938. "Thalassa: A Theory of Genitality." London, England: Marsfield Library.
Ferenczi, S. 1988. "The Clinical Diary of Sándor Ferenczi," edited by Judith Dupont. Cambridge, Massechusetts; London, England: Harvard University Press.
———. Feb. 2,1932a. "A Dilemna of Mutual Analysis," 28-29.
———. Feb. 21,1932. "Fragmentation," 38-40.
———. May 10,1932. "Traumatic Self Strangulation," 102-106.
———. July 30, 1932, "Literal" Repetition Endlessly Repeated and No Recollection, 179-184.
Foucault, M. "In: Eros, F. 2004. The Ferenczi Cult; Its Historical and Political Roots," *International Forum of Psychoanalysis*, Vol. 13, 122-128.
Freud, A. 1974, "IntroductionTo Psychoanalysis: Lectures for Child Analysts and Teachers. In *The Writings of Anna Freud 1922-1935, Vol. 1*, New York: International Universities Press, Inc.
Freud, A. 1966[1936]. "The Ego And The Mechanism Of Defense." Vol. 2, New York: International Universities Press, Inc.
———. 1971. "Forward to The Wolf-Man's Memoirs, the Case Studies by Freud and Ruth Mack Brunswick." In *The Wolf-Man by the Wolf–Man*, ix-xii. New York: Basic Books, Inc.
Freud, S. 1893–1895. "Studies on Hysteria." S.E., 2.
———. 1900. "The Interpretation of Dreams." S.E., 4.
———. 1905a[1901]. "Fragment of an Analysis of a case of hysteria." S.E.,7.
———. 1905b. Three Essays On The theory Of Sexuality. S.E., 7.
———. 1909a. "Analysis of a Phobia in a Five-Year-Old Boy. S.E., 10.
———. 1909b. "Notes Upon a Case of Obsessional Neurosis." S.E.,10.
———. 1910a. "Leonardo Da Vinci And A Memory Of His Childhood." S.E. XI.
———. 1910b. "A Special Type of Choice Made by Men" (Contributions to the Psychology of Love). S.E., 11.
———. 1912. "The Dynamics of Transference." S.E., 12.
———. 1913a. "Totem and Taboo." [1912-1913]. S.E.,13.
———. 1913b. "On Beginning the Treatment (Further Recommendations on the Technique of Psycho-Analysis I)." S.E.,12.
———. 1914a. "Remembering, Repeating and Working-Through (Further Recommendations on the Technique of Psych-Analysis III)." S.E.,12.
———. 1914b. "On Narcissism: An Introduction." S.E., 14.
———. 1915[1914]a. "Observations on Transference-Love (Further Recommendations on the Technique of Psycho-Analysis III." S.E.,12.
———. 1915b. "Instincts and their Vicissitudes." S.E., 14.
———. 1916a. "Some Thoughts On Development and Regression-Aetiology." S.E., 16.
———. 1916b. "The Libido Theory and Narcissism." S.E.,16.

———. 1917 [1915]. "Mourning and Melancholia." S.E., 14.
———. 1918[1917]. "The Taboo of Virginity (Contributions to the Psychology of Love, III)." S.E.,11.
———. 1918. "From the History of an Infantile Neurosis." S.E.,17.
———. 1920a. "The Psychogenesis of a Case of Homosexuality in a Woman." S.E.,18.
———. 1920b. "Beyond the Pleasure Principle." S.E.,18.
———. 1921. "Group Psychology and the Analysis of the Ego." S.E.,18.
———. 1923. "The Ego and the Id." S. E.,19.
———. 1926[1925]. "Inhibitions, Symptoms and Anxiety." S. E., 20.
———. 1927. "The Future of An Illusion." S.E. 21.
———. 1930[1929]. "Civilization And Its Discontents." S.E. 21.
———. 1937a. "Analysis Terminable and Interminable." S.E. 23.
———. 1937b. "Constructions in Analysis." S.E. 23.
———. 1940[1938]. Splitting of the Ego in the Process of Defense. S.E., 23.
———. 1950[1895]. "Project for a Scientific Psychology." S. E.1. Uber "Wilde" Psychoanalyse. *Zentralblatt fur Psychoanalyse*, Jahrig. 1. S. 94.
Freud, S. 1956. Collected Papers-Translated by Joan Riviere, Vol. 3. London: Hogarth Press And The Institute of Psychoanalysis.
Freud, S. 1974. *The Standard Edition Of The Complete Psychological Works Of Sigmund Freud*, edited by James Strachey.Vol. 1-24, 1971. London: Hogarth Press And The Institute Of Psychoanalysis.
Fromm, E. 1963. *Psychology and Culture*. New York: Holt, Rhinehart & Winston.
Gardiner, M. 1971. "The Wolf-Man by the Wolf-Man," edited by Muriel Gardiner. New York: Basic Books, Inc.
Gay, P. 1988. "Freud: A Life of Our Time." New York: W.W. Norton & Company.
———. 1998. "Pleasure Wars: the Bourgeoise Experience Victoria To Freud." New York/ London: W.W. Norton & Company.
Glenn, J. 1980. "Freud's Adolescent Patients: Katrina, Dora, and the Homosexual Woman." *Freud and His Patients*, edited by M. Kanzer & J. Glenn, 23-47, Vol. II. Downstate Psychoanalytic Institute. New York/London: Jason Aronson.
Glover, E. 1933. "Review of the Psycho-Analysis of Children by Melanie Klein." *International Journal of Psycho-Analysis*, 14:119-29.
———. 1937. "Unconscious Functions of Education." In *The Early Development of Mind*, 1956, 283-289. New York: International Universities Press.
———. 1938. "The Psychoanalysis of Affects." In *Selected Papers on Psychoanalysis, Vol.1*, 1956, Edward Glover. New York: International Universities Press.
———. 1945. "An Examination of the Klein System of Child Psycholgy." *Psychoanalytic Study of the Child, Vol.1*:75-117. New York: International Universities Press.
Green, A. 2000. "The Chains In Psychoanalysis." London: Karnac.
Greenacre, P. 1958. "Emotional Growth, Vol. II. New York: International Universities Press.
Greenberg, J.R. and Mitchell, S.A. 1983. "Object Relations in Psychoanalytic Theory." Cambridge, Massachusetts/London, England: Harvard University Press.
Greenberg, J.R. 1991. "Oedipus and Beyond: A Clinical Theory." Cambridge, Massachusetts/ London, England: Harvard University Press.
———. 1999 [1986]. "Theoretical Models and the Analyst's Neutrality." In *Relational Psychoanalysis: The Emergence of a Tradition*, edited by Mitchell, S. & Arons, L. London, England/Hillsdale, NJ.: The Analytic Press.
Grosskurth, P. 1987. "Melanie Klein: Her World And Her Work." Cambridge: Harvard University Press.
Grotstein, J. and Rinsley, D.B. 1994. "Fairbairn and the Origins of Object Relations," edited by Grotstein, J. and Rinsley, D.B., New York and London: Guilford Press.
Guntrip, H. 1961a. "Author's Preface." In *Personality Structure And Human Interaction*,17-18. New York: International Universities Press, Inc.
———. 1961b. "Psychology and Psychoanalysis." In *Personality Structure And Human Interaction*. 34-42. New York: International Universities Press, Inc.

———. 1961c. "The Later Freudian Structural Theory and Analysis of the Ego." In *Personality Structure And Human Interaction*, 89-100. New York: International Universities Press, Inc.

———. 1961d. "Process Theory and Personal Theory." In *Personality Structure And Human Interaction*, 118-160. New York: International Universities Press, Inc.

———. 1961e. "The Relation of Melanie Klein's Work to Freud." In *Personality Structure and Human Interaction*,192-214. New York: International Universities Press, Inc.

———. 1961f. "The Psychodynamic Theory of Melanie Klein." In *Personality Structure And Human Interaction*, 215-233. International Universities Press, Inc.

———. 1961g. "The Basic Forms of Human Relationship." In *Personality Structure And Human Interaction*, 353-379. New York: International Universities Press, Inc.

———. 1969a[1952]. "The Schizoid Personality and the External World." In *Schizoid Phenomena Object–Relations And The Self*,17-48. New York: International Universities Press, Inc.

———. 1969b[1961]. "The Schizoid Problem, Regression and the Struggle to Preserve an Ego." In *Schizoid Phenomena Object-Relations And The Self*, 49-86. New York: International Universities Press.

———. 1969c[1963]. "Four Phases of Psychodynamic Theory." In *Schizoid Phenomena Object-Relations And The Self*, 117-129. New York: International Universities Press, Inc.

Hartmann, H. 1958[1939]. *Ego Psychology and the Problem of Adaptation*. New York: International Universities Press, Inc.

Hartmann, H., Kris, E. & Loewenstein, R. 1953. "The Function of Theory in Psychoanalysis." In *Drives, Affects, Behavior, Loewenstein, Vol. I*, 13-37. New York: International Universities Press, Inc.

Haynal, A. 2012. "Ferenczi Now and Then: An Introduction to His World." In *Ferenczi and His World: Rekindling the Spirit of the Budapest School*, edited by J. Szekacs–Weisz and T. Keve, 69-86. London: Karnac.

Heimann, P. 1991[1943]. "Some Aspects of the Role of Introjection and Projection In Early Development." In *The Freud-Klein Controversies 1941-45*, edited by Pearl King & Ricardo Steiner. London: Routledge & The Institute of Psychoanalysis.

Hidas, A. 2012. "Ferenczi and Trauma: A Perilous Journey To the Labyrinth." In *Ferenczi And His World: Rekindling the Spirit Of the Budapest School*, edited by J. Szekacs-Weisz and T. Keve, 111-128. London: Karnac.

Horney, K. 1950. "Neurosis and Human Growth." New York: W.W. Norton & Company.

Isaacs, S. 1991[1943]. "The Nature and Function of Phantasy." In *The Freud-Klein Controversies 1941-45*. London: Routledge & The Psychoanalytic Institute.

Isakower, O. 1936. 'Beitrag zur Pathoppsychologie der Einschlaphanomene,' *International Zeitschrift fur Psychanalyse*, 22:466-77.

Jacobson, E. 1964. "The Self and the Object World," Madison: International Unversities Press, Inc.

Janet, P. 1888. 'Les actes inconscients et la memoire,' Rev. phil.,13.

Jones, E. 1909, "Nov. 24 Address To the Niagara District Association at St. Catherine, Ontario, Canada. The Psychoanalytic Method of Treatment." In *Papers On Psycho-Analysis*, 1918. London: Bailliere, Tindall and Cox.

———. 1911, "The Therapeutic Effect Of Psycho-Analysis. Read Before The Detroit Society of Neurology and Psychiatry, 300-311." In *Papers On Psycho-Analysis*, 1918. London: Bailliere, Tindall and Cox.

———. 1911, May 16. "The Psychology Of Every Day Life. Address Before The Detroit Academy of Medicine," 40-103. In *Papers On Psycho-Analysis*, 1918. London: Bailliere, Tindall and Cox.

———. 1957[1935]. "Critique of The Death Instinct." In *The Life and Work of Sigmund Freud*, Vol. 3. New York: Basic Books.

———. 1952. In *Psychoanalytic Studies Of The Personality*, Fairbairn, Preface, v. London: Routledge & Kegan Paul.

———. 1953, 1955, 1957. *The Life and Work Of Sigmund Freud. Vol. I, II, III*. New York: Basic Books.

———. 1957. Freud - Letter to 'Committee,' 1924. Vol. III. 197-198.

———. 1957. Freud letter to Ferenczi, Vol. III. Jan. 22, 1924.

———. 1957. Freud letter to Jones, Vol. III, 1927, 197-198.

Kandel, E. 1998. "A New Intellectual Framework for Psychiatry." *American Journal of Psychiatry*, 155:457-469.

Kanzer, M. & Glenn, J. 1980. "Freud and His Patients," edited by Kanzer, M. & Glenn, J. Vol. II, Downstate Psychoanalytic Institute. New York/London: Jason Aronson.

Kanzer, M. 1980. "Dora's Imagry: the Flight From a Burning House." In *Freud and His Patients*, edited by Kanzer, M. & Glenn, J., 72-81. Downstate Twenty-Fifth Anniversary Series. New York/London: Jason Aronson.

Kernberg, O. 2011. "Divergent, Contemporary Trends in Psychoanalytic Theory." *Psychoanalytic Review*, 98: 632-664.

King, P. and Steiner, R., 1991. *The Freud-Klein Controversies, 1941-1945*. London: Routledge.

Klein, M. 1921. "The Development of a Child." In *Melanie Klein: Love, Guilt and Reparation and Other Works 1921-1945*, 1-53. New York: The Free Press, A Division of Macmillan, Inc.

———. 1923. "Early Analysis. " In *Melanie Klein: Love, Guilt and Reparation and Other Works 1921-1945*, 77-105. New York: The Free Press, A Division of Macmillan, Inc.

———. 1925. "A Contribution To the Psychogenesis of Tics." In *Love, Guilt and Reparation and Other Works, 1921-1945*, 106-127. 1975. New York: The Free Press, A Division of Macmillan, Inc.

———. 1926. *The Psychological Principle of Early Analysis*.

———. 1927. "Symposium on Child Analysis." In *Love, Guilt and Reparation and Other Works 1921-1945*, 139-167.1975. New York: The Free Press, A Division of Macmillan, Inc.

———. 1933. "The Early Development of Conscience in a Child." In *Love, Guilt and Reparation and Other Works 1921-1945*, 248-257.1975. New York: The Free Press, A Division of Macmillan, Inc.

———. 1935. "A Contribution to the Psychogenesis of Manic Depressive States." In *Love, Guilt and Reparation and Other Works 1921-1945*, 262-289. 1975. New York: The Free Press, A Division of Macmillan, Inc.

———. 1945. "The Oedipus Complex in the Light of Early Anxieties." In *Love, Guilt and Reparations and Other Works 1921-1954*, 370-419.1975. New York: The Free Press, A Division of Macmillan, Inc.

———. 1948. "On The Theory of Anxiety and Guilt." In *Envy and Gratitude and Other Works 1946-1963*, 25-42. New York: The Free Press, A Division of Macmillan, Inc.

———. 1952a. "The Origins Of Transference." In *Envy and Gratitude and Other Works 1946-1963*, 25-42. 1975. New York: The Free Press, A Division of Macmillan, Inc.

———. 1952b. "The Mutual Influences in the Development of Ego and Id." In *Envy and Gratitude and Other Works 1946-1963*, 57-60. 1975. New York: The Free Press, A Division of Macmillan, Inc.

———. 1952c. "Some Theoretical Conclusions Regarding the Emotional Life of the Infant." In *Envy and Gratitude and Other Works 1946-1963*, 61-93. 1975. New York: The Free Press, A Division of Macmillan, Inc.

———. 1952d. "On Observing the Behaviour of Young Infants." In *Envy and Gratitude And Other Works 1946-1963*, 94-123.1975. New York: The Free Press, A Division of Macmillan ,Inc.

———. 1955a. "On Identification." In *Envy and Gratitude and Other Works 1946-1963*, 141-175. 1975. New York: The Free Press, A Division of Macmillan, Inc.

———. 1957. "Envy and Gratitude." In *Envy and Gratitude And Other Works 1946-1963*, 176-235.1975. New York: The Free Press, A Division of Macmillan, Inc.

———. 1958. "On the Development of Mental Functioning." In *Envy and Gratitude And Other Works*, 236-246.1975. New York: The Free Press, A Division of Macmillan, Inc.

———. 1961[1945]. "Narative of a Child Analysis." London, England: Hogarth Press.

Kraft–Ebing R. 1886 *Psychopatia Sexualis: Eine klinisch-forensisch*. Studie, Stuttgart: Ferdinand Enke.

Kurzweil, E. 1998 [1989]. "The Freudians: A Comparative Perspective." New Haven: Yale University Press.

———. 2012. "Ferenczi In Context." In *Ferenczi And His World: Rekindling the Spirit of the Budepest School*, edited by Judit Szekacs-Weisz and Tom Keve, 55-68. London: Karnac.

Laplanche, J. 1970. "Life & Death." In *Psychoanalysis*. Baltimore: The John Hopkins University Press.

———. 2015. *The Temptation of Biology: Freud's Theories of Sexuality*. New York: The Unconscious in Translation.

Laplanche, J. and Pontalis, J.B., 1973. "The Language of Psychoanalysis." New York: W.W. Norton and Company.

Loewald H. 1951. "Ego As Reality." *International Journal of Psycho-analysis*, Vol. 32:10-18.

———. 1978. "Instinct Theory, Object Relations, Psychic-Srructure Formation." *Journal of The American Psychoanalytic Association*, 26:496-503.

———. 1980 [1971]. "On Motivation and Instinct Theory." In *Papers in Psychoanalysis*, 207-218. New Haven: Yale University Press.

Lussier, A. 1988. "The Limitations of the Object Relations Model." *Psychoanalytic Quarterly*, 57:528-546.

Makari, G. 2008. *Revolution In Mind: The Creation of Psychoanalysis*. Harper Collins.

Meynert, T. 1889. "Beitrag zum Verstandnisse der traumatischen Neurosen." Wien. klin. Wschr.,2.

Mitchell, S. A. 1981. "The Origin and Nature of the 'object' in the Theories of Klein and Fairnbairn." *Contemporary Psychoanalysis*, 17:374-398.

———. 1998. "Relational Concepts In Psychoanalysis: An Integration." Cambridge: Harvard University Press.

Modell, A. 1990. "Other Times, Other Realities: Toward a Theory of Psychoanalytic Treatment." Cambridge/London: Harvard University Press.

Moll, A. 1891. *Die contrare Sexualempfindung*. Berlin: Fischer's Medicinische Buchhandlung, H. Korneld.

Ogden, T.H. 1986. "The Matrix of the Mind: Object Relations and the Psychoanalytic Dialogue." Northvale, New Jersey: Jason Aronson.

———. 2002. "A New Reading of Object-Relations Theory." *International Journal of Psychoanalysis*, 83: 767-782.

Pankseep, J. 1998. "Affective Neuroscience: The Foundations of Human and Animal Emotions." New York: Oxford University Press.

Paskauskas, R. Andrew. 1993. *The Complete Correspondence of Sigmund Freud and Ernest Jones, 1908-1939*. Cambridge: Harvard University Press.

———. Freud letter to Jones, May 31,1927.

Phillips, A. (1988). "Winnicott." Cambridge: Harvard University Press.

Poland, W. 2002. "Psycholgy In the Culture." *Journal of the American Psychoanalytic Association*, Vol. 50: 1103-1108.

Rangel, L. 2002. "The Theory of Psychoanalysis: Vicissitudes of Its Evolution." *Journal of the American Psychoanalytic Association*, Vol. 50:1109-1132.

Rapaport, D. 1951. "The Conceptual Model of Psycoanalysis." In *The Collected Writings of David Rapaport*, edited by M. Gill. New York: Basic Books, Inc.

Reiser, M. 1985. "Converging Sectors of Psychoanalysis and Neurobiology: Mutual Challenges and Opportunity." *Journal of the American Psychoanalytic Association*, 33:11-34.

Roazen, P. 2001. "The Historiography Of Psychoanalysis." U.S.A. London: Tranaction Publisher.

Rodman, F.R. 2003a. "Winnicott: Life and Work." Cambridge: Perseus.

———. 2003b (Nov. 1952) "Letter to Klein." In *Winnicott: Life and Work*. Cambridge: Perseus.

Ross, J.M., 2007. "Trauma, Abuse in the Case of Little Hans: A Contemporary Perspective." *Journal Of The American Psychoanalytic Association*, Vol. 3, pp. 779-798.

Sandler, J., and Rosenblatt, B. 1962. "The Concept of the Representational World." *Psychoanayltic Study of the Child*, 17:128-145. New York: International Universities Press.

Schafer, R. 1983. "The Analytic Attitude." New York: Basic Books Inc.

———. 1997. "The Contemporary Kleinians of London." In *The Contemporary Kleinians of London*, edited by Schafer, 1-26. Madison: International Universities Press.

Scharfman, M.A. 1980). "Further Reflections on Dora." In *Freud And His Patients*, edited by Kanzer, M. & Glenn, J., Vol. 11, Downstate Twenty-Fifth Anniversary Series, 48-57. New York/London: Jason Aronson.

Schwartz, C. (1989). "Ambivalence: Its Relationship to Narcissism and Superego Development." *Psychoanalytic Review*, 76:511-521.

———. 1998. "Freud's Treatment of the Rat Man: A Polemic with His Critics." *Psychoanalytic Review*, 85:373-397.

Shapiro, T. 1990. "Unconscious Fantasy: Introduction." *Journal of the American Psychoanalytic Association*, 38:36-46.

Steiner, R. 1991. "Background to the Scientific Controversies." In *The Freud-Klein Controversies 1941-1945*, 227-263. London: Routledge.

Stolorow and Atwood. 1992. *Context of Being*. Hilldale, NJ: The Analytic Press.

Stone, L. 1971. "Reflections on the Psychoanalytic Concept of Aggression." *Psychoanalytic Quarterly*, 40:195-244.

Strachey, J. 1950 [1895]. "Intoduction to: Project For a Scientific Psychology." In *The Standard Edition Of The Complete Psychological Works Of Sigmund Freud*, edited by J. Strachey, 283-293, S.E. 1.

Stuart, J. (2007). "Hans and Freud's Self Analysis: A Biographical View of Clinical Theory in the Making." *Journal Of The American Psychoanalytic Association*, Vol. 55.

———. 2007. "Postscript: Restructuring Our Collective Past." *Journal of the American Psychoanalytic Association, Vol. 3*, 851-852.

Vorus, N. 2001. "The Concept of Phantasy in Psychoanalysis: An Examination of the Place of Reality." In *The Freud–Klein Controversies 1941-1945*. London: Routledge.

Wakefield, J.C. 1990. "Is Freud's Concept of Instinct Incoherent? Resolving Strachey's Dilemna." *Psychoanalytic Contemporary Thought*, Vol. 13:241-262.

———. 2007. "Attachment and Sibling Rivalry In Little Hans: The Fantasy Of The Two Giraffas Revisited." *Journal of the American Psychoanalytic Association*, Vol. 55, 821-850.

Winnicott, D. W. 1957 [1939] "Aggression." In *The Child and the Outside World*, edited by Janet Hardenberg, 167-175. London: Tavistock Publications Limited.

———. 1957a [1942.] "Why Children Play." In: *The Child and the Outside World*, edited by Janet Hardenberg, 149-152. London: Tavistock Publications Limited.

———. 1957b [1945]. "Towards An Objective Study of Human Nature." In *The Child and the Outside World*, edited by Janet Hardenberg, 125-133. London: Tavistock Publications Limited.

———. 1957c [1947]. "Further Thoughts on Babies As Persons." In: *The Child and the Outside World*, edited by Janet Hardenberg,134-140. London: Tavistock Publications Limited.

———. 1957d [1954]. "Breast Feeding." In: *The Child and the Outside World*, edited by Janet Hardenberg, 141-14. London: Tavistock Publications Limited.

———. 1958a. "Psychoanalysis and the Sense of Guilt." In: *Maturational Processes and the Facilitating Environment,1965*,15-28. New York: International Universities Press.

———. 1958b. "The Capacity To Be Alone." *Maturational Processes and the Facilitating Environment,1965*. 29-36. New York: International Universities Press, Inc.

———. 1960. "Ego Distortion in Terms of True and False Self." In *The Maturational Process and the Facilitating Environment, 1965*,140-152. New York: International Universities Press, Inc.

———. 1962a. "Ego Integration in Child Development. In *Maturational Process And the Facilitating Environment, 1965*, 56-63. New York: International Universities Press.

———. 1962b. "A Personal View of the Kleinian Contribution." In *The Maturational And The Facilitating Environment, 1965*,171-178. New York: International Universities Press.

———. 1963a. "From Dependence Towards Independence in the Development of the Individual." In *The Maturational Process And The Facilitating Environment, 1965*, 83-92. New York: International Universities Press.

———. 1963b. “Morals and Education.” In *The Maturational Process And The Facilitating Environment,1965*, 83-92. New York: International Universities Press.

———. 1963c. “Communicating and Not Communicating Leading to a Study of Certain Opposites.” In *The Maturational and the Facilitating Environment, 1965*, 179-192. New York: International Universities Press.

———. 1971 [1951]) The Transitional Object and Transitional Phenomena. In *Playing and Reality*. New York: Basic Books.

———. 1989 [1959]. “The Fate of the Transitional Object.” In *Psychoanalytic Explorations: D.W. Winnicott*, edited by Clare Winnicott, Ray Shepherd & Madeleine Davis, 53-58. Cambridge Massschusetts: Harvard University Press.

———. 1989 [1966]. “The Split-off Male and Female Elements to Be Found in Men and Women.” In *Psychoanalytic Explorations: D.W. Winicott*, edited by Clare Winicott, Ray Shepherd & Madeleine Davis,1989, 170-182. New York: International Universities Press.

Young-Breuhl, E. 1988. “Anna Freud: A Biography.” New York: Summit.

———. Letter by Freud to Max Ettinger,1927, fn. 58, ch.4.

Index

About the Author

Charlotte Schwartz, LCSW, is a psychoanalyst and author in West Palm Beach, Florida. She is formerly assistant professor of pediatrics at New York Medical College, supervisor of Treatment Services and Social Work Training, and adjunct professor at Smith College School for Social Work. She is a member of the International and American Psychoanalytic Societies and training and supervisory analyst at the National Psychological Association for Psychoanalysis. She is co-editor of *Sexual Faces*, and author of numerous articles.

www.ingramcontent.com/pod-product-compliance
Ingram Content Group UK Ltd.
Pitfield, Milton Keynes, MK11 3LW, UK
UKHW041122071026
15587UKWH00009B/98

9 781498 568487